PEACEANGEL'S
WHITE FEATHERS

Norah Brown-Davis

PEACEANGEL'S WHITE FEATHERS

PEACEANGEL'S WHITE FEATHERS

BY NORAH BROWN-DAVIS

StoryTerrace

I would like to dedicate this book to my three children, who have sharpened my brain over the years, and helped me along my questioning journey.

Text Judy Brown, on behalf of Story Terrace

Design Grade Design and Adeline Media, London

Copyright © Norah Brown-Davis & Story Terrace

Text is private and confidential

First print January 2019

StoryTerrace

www.StoryTerrace.com

CONTENTS

INTRODUCTION

 story of one woman's life, through an evangelical

upbringing and the ups and downs of life, including death, widowhood, questioning and finding worth as a person.

When I started writing these memoirs, I found myself hesitating, as what I wanted to say might seem to come across as a kind of shock to people who, throughout my childhood, thought they were guiding me in a Christian way. That way was straight, narrow and walled-in by rules. But now it occurs to me that I was the one who was subsequently shocked by these attitudes, which to them seemed normal and desirable – shocked into asking questions.

Here I am at 70, feeling like I'm up in the sky, looking down on my life here on earth. So what do I see? A female first-born child born in 1946 to an Irish/Ulster-Scots couple, whose families had both been immersed in a Christian denomination called 'The Brethren'. In many ways the Brethren defined their lives. I daresay this was for the good in some respects, though not, in my opinion, in all. Undoubtedly my parents loved me and my brother and intended to bring us up in the ways impressed on them by their own parents. But views and beliefs are not cast in stone, nor something you inherit in your genes, and I went on asking questions. Questions like: How do you know you are right? Who is this God? Who am I really? In the end though, I moved away to some extent from our parents' mode of thinking. Just as my children have done. You could call it growing up.

Now, 70 years later, I look back on a young life full of wonder, curiosity, disappointment, joy and yes, worship of our creator God. I wanted to know about everything: nature, literature, performing arts, foreign countries, art. My curiosity earned me the nickname 'Nosey Norah' and I became fascinated with people from other lands, philosophy, books, genealogy, the human body, the whole sex thing. And for me there was always music and worship, and worship through making music.

Now it is 2017. It is 35 years since the night my husband Chris died and I thought my world had ended. I have awoken in the night and, as I often do, I have turned on the bedside radio. It is tuned to BBC Radio 4. When I press the button twice it stays on for 90 minutes, three times for 60 minutes, four for 30, five for 15. This is how I deal with insomnia. My bladder tells me I need to get up. The programme interests me. As I am now living alone again with nobody else trying to get to sleep in the house, I turn up the volume so I don't miss the talk. It's about finding an ancient hobbit-like skull, thousands of years old. That reminds me of a conversation I had with Chris about Tolkien's hobbits back before we were married. The previous programme was a fast and heated discussion on the Greek economy with the Greek Chancellor of the Exchequer: he was maintaining he was right, the interviewer interspersing rapid questions and responses. It's the sort of thing I like about Radio 4: intelligent, fast, well-recorded discussion. Chris enjoyed radio too. How I admired his intelligence, his ability to argue logically, discuss current affairs, write excellent papers on science, economics and current affairs. He had been at university before we met, and spent a short time with the Health Service writing his master's degree paper on public attitudes to cancer. Next, he wrote a brief newspaper

8

article on Ian Paisley and Northern Ireland politics. Then the desire to start his own business in insulation technology took shape. Polystyrene insulation was a cutting-edge idea back then in 1976: the granules were pumped into cavity walls to prevent heat escape, while mineral wool was used in jackets for hot-water cylinders. The oil crisis had just begun, and prices for petrol and heating oil were rocketing.

By now it is 3.21am I decide to turn on my tablet and write this blog. At 4.21am the radio switches itself off. Immersed in my memories, I have lost track of the discussion programme.

Meeting Chris's family back in 1967-8, I loved the way they talked at mealtimes about politics, religion and world topics in a way my family never did. My father was an intelligent man, but quiet and very reserved. A professional engineer, he found his work absorbing and his faith satisfying.

My mother was also intelligent, but was held back from expressing her views by the fashion of the day, especially in church circles, where it was not considered fitting for women to contribute to debate. As for me, I wished I had been given the chance to go to university instead of going straight into a nursing career like other women in our family. I discovered later that my parents felt university would have given me too many opportunities to ask questions, and that was not deemed appropriate for a Brethren girl like me. Chris's brother Terence had studied at Trinity College, Dublin, studying literature and philosophy. He married an American student there the same year that we married. To me, this family opened up a whole new world, and I was very much in love with it, and with Chris.

There was a soft, gentle side to Chris as well. He was a good father, not very confident at the baby stage, but loving it once the children started talking. He apparently had not talked until he was about four, when he started straight into full sentences. Our daughter Jenny adored him and is the one who remembers most about him and grieves most for his loss.

Chris and I were both 23 when we married. We had 14 years of happy marriage, and it is now 35 years since he died. I have made the best of the life I have been left with. Thanks to Chris I have three healthy children, grown into fine, intelligent adults, all like him in different ways, and missing him each in their own way, whether or not they are aware of it. Jonathan looks most like him. Though, never having consciously known his father, he does not realise how much he has inherited from him. Niall is more like Chris in temperament and, being a middle child, is the easiest for me to relate to. Jenny has his brain – well, they all do, but she remembers him best and is still deeply grieving for the dad she adored. They all remind me of his ability to explore and research new ideas.

The question 'Why?' is always present. Yes, I have made the best I could of the life I was left, but how different it could have been, had he lived. I adored him for the 14 years we had together. And I miss him terribly even now. Other relationships have been interesting, but few come close to what we had. I constantly go through theories about why he died and how God could have allowed it. Was it the Dublin Bay prawn cocktails he loved, which might have absorbed chemicals from Sellafield into his system? Was it his mother's placental insufficiency, considering she had returned from China in 1945, pregnant, but extremely underweight and suffering from tropical sprue?

My Christian faith has never left me, although I have had serious questions over the years. My church (now Non-subscribing Presbyterian) supported me greatly during my early widowhood, and I appreciated that. But, for the children, religion has rung hollow. None of them have continued to have a faith, and I myself have sometimes struggled. Life goes on regardless. Perhaps someday we will   all   understand.

1
A BRETHREN UPBRINGING

Parents and Grandparents

My mother's family were a strong influence in my young life. I had an array of aunts, great-aunts, uncles and cousins, most of them living in or around Belfast and all of them with a ready welcome for my brother Arthur and me.

My mother Muriel, her sisters Doris and Myra and her brother Cecil were the children of Jack and Norah Wilson of Ballina, Co Mayo, where Jack managed a prosperous hardware store. Doris and Muriel were born in Dublin, and Myra and Cecil in Ballina. They lived in a large detached house with an extensive garden on the outskirts of the town. My grandfather Jack started up the Ballina branch of the Brethren. Grandmother Norah sometimes went to other churches as well; she liked company and found a good circle of friends that way. She enjoyed music and acquired a gramophone with a set of His Master's Voice records. Her best friend was Mrs Duncan, whose husband was editor of the Ballina Herald. Mr and Mrs Duncan often invited the Wilson family for Sunday lunch at their house on Main Street, and decades later the rich enticing smell of roast beef would transport my mother Muriel back to those feasts. Even more fascinating to the small Wilsons was the talking parrot, who lived in a large cage in Mrs Duncan's kitchen. And every

Christmas, Mrs Duncan cleared her drawing room and turned it into a showroom of toys for sale. The Wilson children got first pick.

My mother recalled idyllic family holidays at a cottage in Enniscrone where, as small children, the sisters and Cecil would play for days on end on the beach and among the sand hills. They called the largest of the Enniscrone dunes 'The Valley of Diamonds' because of the beautiful pearlised shells they found in its hollows.

Some years, Norah used to take the children to Ross near Castlebar for the summer months. They took their beds with them, and oil-fired ovens for baking bread. They would all, even little Cecil, walk from Ross to Rathfran for the day, bringing a picnic lunch. But one day at Ross, Norah was bitten by an ant. The bite didn't heal properly, even when they went home. It must have poisoned her, as she didn't seem well all autumn. One bitter November day she caught a chill while outside hanging the washing on the line, then picked up a cold which turned to pneumonia. She was ill for a week. Doris, the eldest sister, was away at the time, and it was Muriel whom Norah called for on the night she died. It was 10pm on 22nd November 1932, and Muriel was 12 and a half.

On the day of the funeral, Norah's brother Harry came from Dublin and took the children for a walk while the hearse left the house. His wife didn't come. However, a succession of other aunts arrived to look after the family over the following months. At Christmas, it was Jack's unmarried sister Lila who came to stay. The Wilson children didn't like their Aunt Lila's cooking much, especially when they discovered she had chopped the turkey liver, heart, etc. and put them in the stuffing. Next, Norah's sister, their Aunt Florrie, arrived with her younger daughter Dorrie. Cousin Dorrie was a scamp and very obstreperous.

My grandfather Jack found strength and solace through his church. He had been born into and brought up in the Presbyterian tradition, but along the way was influenced by the Brethren, a Protestant non-conformist sect originating in Dublin in the late 1820s. It was similar to but less strict than the Plymouth Brethren in Devon. Jack and Norah had both adopted Brethren beliefs, even though Jack's parents disapproved so strongly that they disinherited him on its account. He, Norah and the children used to troop along to meetings at the local Gospel hall he had set up, where the Gospel was preached with great urgency and enthusiasm but without the trappings of prayer books, formal creed or grand buildings. The area of Mayo where they lived was mainly Catholic; Presbyterians were a minority and the Brethren were even less well-known. However, they presented the Gospel with freshness and zeal and were keen to convert Catholics to this new approach to Christianity.

When Jack met Ethel Catherwood, he found love again, and also a stepmother for his children. Ethel had no children of her own, but set herself to bringing up her readymade family with great interest and determination.

Ethel's family approved of Jack Wilson. Here is an old letter Ethel received before her marriage from her sister, my great-aunt Hilda Catherwood. My mother, Muriel had kept the letter after her stepmother's death, probably as it was so complimentary about her own mother, Norah, who died so young. I love the gossipy tone.

Dearest Ethel

There was a P.C. from Oban which I need not send on for there was nothing on it except the picture of an old church door and my address, so he isn't huffed yet. I cut the tail off old Peacock however, for I rushed out and did not turn around to speak to him. Fred was as dry as sawdust last night as I must have docked him too at some time! Mother had a good opportunity of telling Edith [Ethel and Hilda's sister, who was to become my paternal grandmother] *about "Moyola" and I think she missed nothing. Amongst other things she said "I used to think I had a lot of nice china but mine is nothing to what she has – some of* the nicest things I have ever seen. The first Mrs W. [my grandmother Norah, née Bollard] *must have been an exceedingly nice person for all her stuff too is so refined and beautiful!! Then the children* [my mum, brother and sisters] *were so clever and lovely etc and Jack* [my grandfather Wilson] *was one of the best and kindest men she ever met without exception, he couldn't be bad for there was no bad in him!" But mother said that to everything she said. Edith* [my Anderson grandmother] *just replied "So I believe!" or "I heard that". As far as I can gather she has heard a good deal. This is about all I can think of. R James (?) was asking for the Free Staters (Irish). I shall probably write again after the 1st Aug. Cheerio in the meantime.*

Fondest love from
Hilda

Later, the Wilson family moved to Strabane. Muriel was not happy there. She missed her Ballina friends but did not want to go to boarding school, so it was decided she should go to Belfast for secretarial training at Ashleigh House School. She stayed in 'digs', as they then called temporary rented accommodation, at Queen Mary's Hostel for Girls on the Lisburn Road. Knowing that Muriel was a shy girl, her stepmother Ethel asked her widowed sister Edith Anderson to invite her out to the family farm at Aghalee in Co Armagh, so that she could meet Edith's five grown-up children. This turned out to be an invitation of destiny, as it was there that Muriel got to know Catherwood Anderson: Edith's son and Ethel's nephew. Catherwood was to become my father.

Edith and William Anderson had begun married life at a farm in Co Tyrone. But William suffered a severe stroke, which left him unable to speak or manage the farm. They moved to Belfast to make life easier for William and to enable their children – Joseph, Catherwood, Hilda, Doreen and Arthur – to get a good education at Methodist College.

My grandmother Edith Anderson (née Catherwood) was a very stern lady. She never gave her grandchildren anything – presents, kisses, nothing! She had given my father the Christian name of 'Catherwood' as that was her maiden name. The Catherwoods came across to me as a wealthy branch of the family, but it later became apparent to me that there were two types of Catherwood: the more religious ones who read and even wrote theological books, and the more secular (and more financially wealthy ones), who had large houses and owned race horses. We were not taken to meet this set – we only ever heard stories about them!

William died in 1934, and without him Edith was not happy in the city. In 1936, after the children had finished school, she bought the farm at Aghalee. Joseph and Catherwood went to work for the Ulster Transport Authority, which had taken over Catherwood Buses, a firm founded by Edith's brother Stewart. Joseph became company secretary while Catherwood studied at Belfast Technical College and became a chartered mechanical engineer with the company. Hilda

16

and Doreen were nurses, and the youngest brother, Arthur, worked on the farm.

Meanwhile, when Ethel brought about the introduction of her pretty step-daughter Muriel to her handsome nephew Catherwood, romance bloomed. So, in a sense my parents, Muriel and Catherwood, met as a kind of arranged marriage. In September 1943 they wed at the Victoria Memorial Hall, a Brethren assembly hall in May Street, Belfast. They spent their honeymoon in Scotland. This did not turn out to be as blissful or carefree as they had hoped, because shy Muriel felt that as newlyweds they were the centre of attention everywhere they went, and she didn't like it. They cut the holiday short and came home to their rented flat in Cranmore Park, a pleasant tree-lined suburb of south Belfast.

The Beginning of Me

On 17th March 1946, I was born at the Massereene Hospital, Antrim, where Catherwood's sister Hilda was matron. It was St Patrick's Day, and they named me Norah Patricia after my maternal grandmother and the saint on whose day I was born.

1946 was also the year of the 'big snow'. I don't remember it, of course, but I have a photo of my father proudly holding me, well 'happed up' in a snowsuit, in our garden at Cranmore Park. Soon afterwards, we moved to Rosetta Parade, which was also in south Belfast.

Three years later, in March 1949, my brother William Arthur Bell Anderson was born. But my mother, Muriel, unfortunately suffered from post-natal depression after having Arthur and remained for a time in the Massereene Hospital under her sister-in-law Hilda's care. It was the first of a series of mental breakdowns she was to suffer. While she and baby Arthur stayed in hospital, I was sent to Aghalee

17

to stay on the farm with my father's family: Grandmother Edith, Aunt Doreen, Uncle Joe and Uncle Arthur. I loved being there, as Doreen was a great cook and made delicious cakes. The farm was a joy to be in. I would collect Beauty of Bath apples in the orchard and go looking for hens' eggs in the hedgerows.

Aunts

And so I started life growing up in a loving family. Although my mother was often ill, having four aunts made up for a lot, and backing them up were uncles, cousins, several great-aunts and a network of other family members. The aunts were my mother's sisters, Doris and Myra, and my father's sisters, Doreen and Hilda.

Now, I believe that everyone should have a crazy aunt. I decided this after reading Graham Greene's novel, Travels with my Aunt. The bachelor nephew in the book, Henry Pulling, is so like some of the men I have known, and they could all do with having an aunt like his Aunt Augusta! As for me, I'm a crazy aunt to Zoe, Sancha, Nik, Michael, Lindsay and Linski, and I had not one but four crazy aunts of my own. Unlike Henry Pulling in the novel, I didn't travel very far in the world with them, but they all influenced me in one way or another. Each in her own way was a little odd, and for fun I have given them craziness scores on a scale of one to 10.

Doris (crazy score: six) was my mother's older sister. After their mother's death, Doris had gone away to train as a nurse at Stoke Mandeville in England, but came back to take a job in Belfast once she had qualified. Here she met and married Robert White, our Uncle Bobbie, a decorator and part-time Brethren preacher. They lived on the Cregagh Road in south Belfast. It was not far from our house, and Arthur and I trotted round there every Wednesday afternoon at three o'clock. Aunt Doris was very motherly, but sadly never had any children of her own. I think she felt it wasn't quite right to investigate why: 'Well, the Lord knows best, doesn't He?' She was especially fond of little boys, so my brother, as her only Northern Irish nephew, was a great favourite – her brother Cecil's daughter and two sons lived in Canada and rarely visited. We would drink tea and eat sweet little tomatoes in season from Uncle Bobbie's greenhouse. I've loved the smell of tomatoes ever since. It was a tiny house, and I had the impression they weren't very well off. Uncle Bobbie was good at drawing and could do nice pencil drawings of animals and children from photographs. I remember they always had copies of National Geographic for us to look at. I suppose I always thought of Aunt Doris as a little mad, as she was less strict than my mother, and would let us get away with things Mum wouldn't. Sadly she died of cancer before I got married, so unfortunately she never met any of my children.

Myra (crazy score: nine) was my mother's younger sister. She was very, very stylish, wore the latest fashions and listened to pop music programmes like Music While You Work on the radio. When she came to visit us, she wore expensive perfumes and gave my mum some of her 'cast-off' designer clothes. She went on exotic holidays to places like the Canary Islands long before they were popular as tourist areas, and she brought me back a basket for my hair ribbons from Las Palmas, which I still have. Myra trained as a nurse but then went to work as manageress of the Rosapenna Hotel in Donegal, which to me as a child sounded exotic and far away. Owned by my grandmother Anderson's brother Stewart, it was built in a Scandinavian style with wooden balconies, and seemed very exciting to me. My mother would phone her there by calling the operator and asking for 'Downings 5, please, a personal call to Myra Wilson'. Auntie Myra married the hotel's French chef, Bernard Voslinski, who was half Russian, half French and very sexy.

Unfortunately, all their wedding presents went up in smoke when the hotel had a fire and was burnt down. They then moved to another exotic hotel in the south of Ireland, Dromoland Castle. After that Bernard wanted to go to America, but unfortunately Myra didn't like it when she got there. I suspect she was not quite as sophisticated as she seemed to me then. She was probably homesick. They also tried living in New Zealand, and though Myra liked it better than America she was still homesick for Ireland. As a compromise they settled for London, where Bernard became CEO of Grand Metropolitan Hotels. This turned out to be very convenient for me as I had been working in London up to the time of my marriage to Chris, and she offered us a couple of nights in the Piccadilly Hotel as part of our honeymoon. More of this later. And sadly, she died there, in somewhat mysterious circumstances.

Doreen (crazy score: three) lived on the home farm at Aghalee and didn't marry until later in life. As I've said, she looked after me when my brother Arthur was born, and throughout our childhood we had many happy times enjoying country life out there. We loved our weekend trips to the farm, when our mother would bring home-made sandwiches and cakes for the family tea, and we used to help with the harvest, collect eggs in a basket (often finding them in nests in the hedgerows), bake cakes and pick apples. I remember being with a small calf in the back of a three-wheeled van, and it sucking my fingers all the way. We filled pails of sweet, fresh well water at the pump, and loved to peep into Uncle Joe's library. This was filled with a great variety of books: Just William, Billy Bunter, The Girls of St Trinian's and Edward Lear's Book of Nonsense, among the heavier theological tomes which I took no interest in at the time.

Hilda (crazy score: seven) was my favourite aunt, though not the craziest. She was a lovely, warm, motherly sort, who sadly never married or had children of her own. My mother told me stories of

20

how she had fallen in love with a Presbyterian minister, but her mother forbade her to marry outside the Christian Brethren. So she dedicated her life to her nursing career, and became matron of the Massereene Hospital in Antrim, where she had a lovely little apartment, with nice crochet throws, Donegal tweed rugs and a collection of Royal Winton 'Hazel' china, which I inherited from her and still have. Sadly, she died from cancer while I was doing my O-levels.

Occasionally, my father would pack us into his Vauxhall 10 and drive the 140 miles to Ballina, Co Mayo, where Muriel's father, Jack, and stepmother, Ethel, lived, and at other times to visit Jack's sisters, our great-aunts Marie (crazy score: 5) and Lila (crazy score: 6), who lived down a long country lane at Kilcairn, Co Armagh. They were both spinsters, and their house was lit by oil lamps and quite gloomy. There were pictures of Highland cattle on the walls, painted by Aunt Marie, and the toilet was in a shed at the end of the garden, with cut-up newspaper for toilet paper. Arthur and I thought it creepy, but our great-aunts used to give us five-shilling crowns or ten-shilling notes, which pleased us and added to our pocket money, so it was worth the long journey and the gloomy house. Our great-aunts were probably sorry for us, as we were regarded as poor on account of our grandfather having been disinherited.

Of my other great-aunts, three more lived in Belfast: Muriel's aunts Mollie and Jeannie Bollard (crazy scores: 3 and 4 respectively) and Hannah Boyd (crazy score: 5). Hannah and her husband James were childless, and Mollie and Jeannie both remained single. Jeannie worked for the Civil Service and Mollie looked after the home. They all shared a large house on the banks of a small glen, where Arthur and I loved to play. It was a strange arrangement: Hannah and James occupied one side of the house, and the two unmarried sisters, Mollie and Jeannie, lived in the room on the other side of the hall.

Great-Aunt Hannah was not as friendly as her two sisters, and we thought she was very stern. We had to sit up straight, without fidgeting, on chairs in the sitting room and drink her bitter brown tea. We preferred the company of the other aunts, who loved small animals and had decorated their living room with pictures of kittens and puppies. They also had a pedal organ and never minded the din we made when we tried to play it. Hannah's husband, James had an old car, which lay rusting in the garage. After his death, Hannah refused to sell it, and would often go and sit in it to remember the good times she had had with him. She eventually allowed my father to take it away and fix it up to working order again.

As for my father, he was clever and capable but very reserved. The sense of love and duty that ruled his life centred on three things: his family, his church and his profession. I have come across a scrappy note he wrote much later in life which, besides intimating that dementia was starting to take hold, shows how he loved his work:

> *Introduced to people, can have lost this new name during further conversation, but remember old names quite well generally. If I try to think out name of person I was introduced, I may get it again later, but not always. I am writing these notes as something comes into my mind, just to get the thoughts down before I forget them. I have always loved my work as a chartered mechanical engineer in Road and Rail Transport County Council Engineer, always aimed to have a responsible and interesting job as a chartered mechanical engineer, but did not mind taking on other work, such as building or electrical requirements but not in detail*

design, but I considered and set out in writing with sketches of my detailed requirements. I very much enjoyed studying and setting down in writing and with sketches my particular requirements any particular job or requirement.

A profession I selected when at school and loved right through to retirement, even with all the changes over the years. Anything new was a challenge to me.

At Home

The Rosetta area of south Belfast was a mixed Catholic/ Protestant area, and our house was a three-storey mid-terrace. My parents rented it to begin with from Mrs Rea, the elderly lady next door, who my parents seemed to know through the church. Her son and daughter-in-law were missionaries in Africa, and I would look forward to their visits, as it meant I could play with their son Harold Rea, who I considered my first boyfriend. I have a touching photo of myself standing with Harold at his grandmother's front door and gazing at him with admiration.

I remember well the clothes we had to wear to keep warm. In those days there was no central heating, only a coal fire in the living room, and occasionally in the 'good room' and even in the bedrooms if it was very cold. My brother and I wore woollen underwear, which tended to shrink in the wash even faster than we grew out of it. I also suffered an old-fashioned contraption known misleadingly as a 'liberty bodice'. It was a thick cotton undergarment with a lot of scratchy seams and rows of fiddly rubber buttons. Sweaters were usually woollen, and itchy. As a teenager I rarely wore trousers, as skirts and stockings were the rule. Stockings were held up with a suspender belt, which left a draughty gap at the waist and top of the legs.

We played in the streets and gardens with the local children of the area. Snow was always fun, and even my father, who didn't often play with us children, would enjoy helping us build a snowman, with coal for eyes and a carrot for a nose. As I grew up and other youngsters invited me to go to the Curzon cinema or theatre with them, I was not allowed. Being middle-class, my parents did not discuss the reasons for our segregation, but I came to learn that I could mix with some families but not others.

Our street, Rosetta Parade, was almost entirely Protestant, as were The Drive and St John's Park nearby. Some neighbours were evangelical, some broad-minded Presbyterian.

The Protestant missionary family next door were reckoned to be acceptable as friends and we were allowed in their house. Another family, who were Protestant but with unknown church affiliation, were deemed fit to give me lifts to school. My friend Denise Suffern came from a Presbyterian family, related to the local Presbyterian minister, who were only partially acceptable due to their connections with the theatre: Denise's uncle produced shows at the Opera House. I was allowed to play with Denise but not to go to plays at the theatre when she invited me. An Italian family was acceptable, but a girl of my own age was not, because my parents considered hers socially inferior. Oddly, there was no problem about Mr and Mrs Montgomery, who were Jehovah's Witnesses. Mrs Montgomery was a singing teacher, but no one was ever invited into her house, which was reputed to be gloriously untidy. The daughter Barbara, who was my own age, was very imaginative and invented a game about children in an orphanage, run by a woman called 'Grillabags'. (Years later, in 2015, I had a visit at my door from some Jehovah's Witnesses. To find something else to talk about, as I was not interested in their brand of religion, I asked did they know a family called Montgomery. Yes, they did, and it appeared the girl I had played with years ago now lived in nearby Newtownards! We made contact through her brother, and eventually we met up with her and her husband. And what a lovely couple they were!)

Rosetta Avenue, however, which had bigger terraced houses, was mainly Catholic. It was out of bounds, and its residents were viewed with disapproval. This was apparently because – I was told – they had large families and didn't know how to stop, and would therefore eventually outnumber the Protestants. Consequently, according to my mother, they couldn't cope with the number of children they did have, so their houses were assumed to be dirty and untidy. They attended the local chapel on the main road, which I was not allowed to go into.

The rules on whom I could and couldn't go around with made no sense to me at all. From an early age I started to question this upbringing, and have continued to do so every day of my life. However, at the time I learned to toe the line and not make too much fuss, as any sort of stress used to send my mother into a nervous breakdown.

Church

Our life centred round our church, Victoria Memorial Hall in May Street, which had once been a music hall but was now a Brethren meeting place. It was not as strict as some other Brethren assemblies, but nonetheless restrictive. The Brethren believed it was wrong to sing anything but hymns on Sundays; wrong to swear; wrong to read novels; wrong to go to the cinema or theatre, listen to pop music or go dancing. Brethren girls should wear their hair long, and not wear trousers or short skirts. Mixing with non-Brethren people was disapproved of. Above all I knew I should never go on a date with anyone who was not of the Brethren. Later, when television was invented, it seemed ages before our parents agreed to buy one. (However, after great pleading we were allowed to watch it in old Mrs Rea's house, if we asked nicely.) My father did eventually buy a TV when he could afford it, but monitored our viewing very strictly. He would bark 'Turn that thing off!' if he didn't like what we were watching.

My brother and I spent a great deal of time attending the Victoria Memorial Hall. We went there three times on Sundays: the morning communion service called 'Breaking of Bread', then Sunday School at 3.30pm and a gospel meeting at night. At the morning service, children had to sit quietly throughout, either with their parents or up in the gallery. It resembled a Quaker service in that there were long silent periods for contemplation, which we found hard to sit through, though there were also hymns from the Redemption Songbook. After dinner my father would take us down on the bus to Sunday School, which took place in the basement of the Memorial Hall. There we learned children's hymns like Jesus Loves Me. At the evening services, things got a bit livelier. It was always a gospel service, to which we were encouraged to bring friends who didn't have a Christian faith in the hope they would 'get saved'. The hymns came from a different book, called Golden Bells, and we sang them with great gusto. One of the lady members of the congregation was renowned for her almost operatic singing voice. I listened to her with awe, but being of a shy disposition I refrained from joining in as she belted out Standing on the Promises of God or some such rousing tune. But I secretly wished I could sing like her. On Friday nights we had Happy Hour, a meeting for children, where we listened to stories, sang gospel songs and/or watched a film. I enjoyed the films – it was the first time I saw time-lapse pictures of flowers opening or clouds scudding across the sky. Our parents approved much more of the friends we made at church, and expected that eventually we would marry one or other of them. But somehow I never felt at ease with the young men at church, and certainly could not imagine marrying any of them.

The ethos of these church meetings was to get everyone 'saved' before Jesus returned to earth. There was some fear engendered that Jesus would come back and take the saved parents but would leave us children behind if we hadn't 'made our decision' before He arrived. And my parents upheld the general belief that the only people who would find themselves in heaven after death would be those who believed exactly the same as they did. So I dutifully made my decision at the tender age of seven, and did actually believe what I was told at the time. Here is a poem I wrote when I was a bit older:

Jesus	*is*	*a*		*perfect*	*friend*
Always	*with*	*me*	*to*	*life's*	*end.*
When	*in*	*trouble*	*he*	*will*	*bide*
By my side.					
Jesus	*loves*	*me,*	*I*	*can*	*tell,*
When	*I*	*read*	*the*	*Bible*	*well.*
God's	*own*	*Son*	*came*	*down*	*from*	*Heaven,*
Saved	*me*	*when*	*I*	*was*	*only*	*seven.*
Now I'm 10!					

A frequent event in Brethren circles was to attend the summer tent meetings, which were held in various places. There was 'The Portstewart Convention', and another gathering 'up the country', which probably meant Co Tyrone. I had no idea where this was, but had to tag along. My brother and I found it intensely boring, the only highlight being the packed lunch in a paper bag. This was home-made sandwiches, 'believers' bread' (a buttered slice of fruit loaf), and a choice of bought sweet cakes, my favourite being two circles of a light cake sandwiched with jam and fresh cream. These meetings had a slightly scary message as the preachers gave lengthy discourses on the need to be saved before the Lord returned to take up to heaven with him all those who had made a definite decision to believe. My attitude then was 'Ho-hum! I don't like this pressure but I'd better hedge my bets and do it.'

Nevertheless, by the time I was about nine or 10 I had begun asking questions. I think it must have been the restrictions on who we could play with that sowed the seeds of doubt and distrust. Also, the scripture lessons at school started me thinking. We were all reading the same Bible stories and singing the same hymns, but the teacher never mentioned having to get saved, and only the Brethren seemed to bother about it. There were other differences too, like celebrating Christmas but not Easter, Harvest Thanksgiving or other religious festivals, and baptising adults by full immersion. I began to distrust the opinions of those whom most people trust implicitly: their family, their church, the belief system they imbibed as a child. I had begun asking questions, in other words, about the big things in life.

However, I never considered myself a rebel. That would be anti-authoritarian, and my father was to me an authoritarian figure – not one to be afraid of, but definitely one to be obeyed. But the main reason I knew I could never rebel against anything was my mother's sadness, which would engulf her and the whole family every few years. There was the constant threat that if any event or person were to rock the boat, disturb the status quo, it would precipitate an emotional breakdown or deep depression affecting every aspect of our family life. So I kept my thoughts to myself, letting them develop and mature until the time was right. Now, at 70, I am pondering why it is that although I grew up in a deeply religious family and was not allowed to ask questions they didn't have an answer to, I rejected their brand of faith but have continued to ask those questions. Over the years I have found some answers, as well as reasons to accept there may not be an answer to all my questions. And I still continue to have a deep faith.

Primary School

To go back a few years in the narrative: my first school was Downey House Preparatory School on Ravenhill Road. It was the prep school for Methodist College, which my father had attended. It was about a mile from our home and, as we had no car at that stage, my father used to walk with me to school. I was a shy child, embarrassed that I could not tie my shoe laces yet, but I made some friends and started to enjoy the lessons. I joined the Brownie pack there, and the music teacher invited me to join the school orchestra. The invitation brought a thrill of pride, as I was beginning to enjoy music. My aunt Myra would sometimes come to visit, and when she did we were allowed to listen to Music While You Work on the wireless. This was much jazzier than the music in our church, and I sensed a certain disapproval from my mother. However, I had never played an instrument, and looked forward to learning something other than the piano, for which I was due to have lessons. But the best the school could offer me, to my disgust, was a triangle.

Maths was a difficult subject for me at that stage, and I remember the maths teacher being very strict to the point of unpleasantness. The school had a swimming pool, and I started learning to swim. But at a school gala, with my mother watching, I slipped under and panicked. I saw my mother panicking too, and by the time they hauled me out I had lost all confidence in the water. I didn't learn to swim properly until I was about 18 years old.

I did enjoy English and nature study, and at the end of my year in Form 2 I was pronounced 'First Girl' in my class. What I liked best were the extensive school grounds, including a small wooded area (which to me seemed enormous) where I liked to play, imagining myself in the sort of stories by Enid Blyton I loved reading.

However, as time went on, I became quite unhappy at Downey House. I was afraid of the maths teacher, and of being bullied on account of my shyness. My marks went down, as did my confidence. One day my father failed to arrive to pick me up (probably due to a misunderstanding of some sort) and I stood crying at the school gate, unsure what to do. In those days, our bread was brought to the door by the bakery delivery man, and he drove past and recognised me as I stood there crying. Unlike now, in those days we were never forbidden to go in a car with a stranger, and in one sense he was no stranger, so I hopped in and was duly delivered home. Events like these, and having to share lessons with a girl in my class whom I did not like, knocked my confidence further. By the next year my marks were down again.

Somehow my parents understood, and although this had been the school of their choice, they could see it was not right for me. After three years there, they moved me to the local primary school, which was within five minutes' walking distance from home. I warmed to my class teacher, the motherly Mrs Brown, who recognised my love of English and introduced me to the joy of reading and writing. Mrs Brown also built up a school choir. We used to sing along to the BBC radio programme, Singing Together. We practised hard, learning songs like My Bonnie Lies over the Ocean and Vair Mi O (the Eriskay Love Lilt) and entered the Belfast Schools 'Singing

Together' competitions at Fisherwick Place in the city centre. And so began my love of music and choral singing. There was also a well-stocked public library housed in the school, and there I developed my love of reading. My marks improved again, and I passed the 11-plus exam with no problem.

Those were very free and easy days: we played in the street with the local children (at least, those we were allowed to play with), inventing our own games and often going farther afield to the brickfields by the Lagan river, or up the Saintfield Road on bicycles, exploring the countryside on our own. One day we found an old train carriage that a farmer had converted into a hen house, but now abandoned, and there we played, happy as could be. I had a bicycle for Christmas one year (second-hand, from the Belfast Telegraph Classified ads) and as I got older, I used to ride out to Bangor on the new Sydenham bypass with my friend Yvonne from Sunday School. One fateful day, my brother had planned to cycle with his friends up to Shaw's Bridge, a beauty spot on the outskirts of Belfast. I was jealous and desperately wanted to go as well, and eventually he reluctantly agreed. So off we set on a beautiful sunny evening, and I was blissfully happy. But perhaps I was over-confident for, as we neared the bridge, my bicycle wheel caught in a hole in the road, and down I went. In a state of shock, though not badly hurt, I was taken into the house of a nearby lady, who decided I needed a shot of brandy. And that was my first taste of alcohol.

Childhood Holidays

We usually took our holidays at the Red House in Portballintrae, where the CSSM Beach Mission supplied our complete entertainment. Sandcastle competitions or bible studies, we loved it. The house was run by a Captain Sharrat, who we thought must have come out of a story book. The hallway of the house was filled with buckets and spades, boots and rain jackets, fishing rods and tackle. In bed, we could hear the sound of the waves crashing on the nearby beach. When the day came to go home, Arthur clung to the railings and refused to leave, as he didn't want to go back home to humdrum everyday life.

Later, when my father worked for the Ulster Transport Authority as a mechanical engineer, we had the privilege of free travel to 'the mainland', as we called Great Britain. Llandudno in Wales and Teignmouth in Devon were our usual haunts. We took the overnight boat from Belfast docks to Heysham, then a train to Crewe and another to our holiday home or hotel. I remember thinking how strange to be walking on a different piece of land from Ireland. It was all part of our education. My parents seemed to enjoy these trips, as we usually stayed in a Christian guest house, with hymn-singing and bible services every evening. In Teignmouth, at age 14, I felt quite grown-up to be mingling with the older girls there. The owner of the guest house often accompanied the hymns on a small concertina, which I wished I could play. Back home in Belfast, I found one in Smithfield Market and set about learning to play. However, it proved harder than I imagined, and I eventually gave up trying.

One year, my father decided to get a caravan, and we towed it down the Irish coast to Brittas Bay in Wicklow. Arthur and I were very excited at the prospect, but sadly my mother did not take to caravanning. It brought on another breakdown, so the caravan was sold. She could not understand why we should want to live in such a small space when we had a perfectly good house at home.

Secondary School

My secondary school was Ashleigh House School in Belfast. My mother had done a secretarial course there, and so she felt it was the place for me. It had a boarding department, but I joined as a day girl. Getting there meant a journey into Belfast centre and out again by a different road, but a neighbour who taught at the school used to offer a lift to me and another girl, leaving us to return by bus. Some of my class had been in the school since their prep-school or even kindergarten days, so they already knew each other and were somewhat cliquish towards the new 11+ entries. Every new girl had to have an interview with the large and daunting headmistress, Miss Welch, who took our history lesson. But after that we rarely saw her, except at morning assembly, when she led the service in majestic style, unaware we were sniggering about the egg and marmalade stains on her ample bosom.

We started in Form 3, which was divided into two classes: A and alpha, A being the brighter pupils who were differentiated by the fact that they studied Latin, while the alpha girls did domestic science. I was chuffed to learn that I was an A pupil, though learning Latin was something I did not particularly enjoy. The English teacher to start with was not a favourite. I didn't like the science teacher either, even though her name was Norah, but I adored the maths and art teachers. My least favourite subject was gym, and hockey was even worse, as we had to play on a cinder pitch and get changed in a draughty shed with no heating. I was also afraid of being hit with the ball, so I did not excel at hockey. Tennis was better, and I really enjoyed that, but netball was my favourite sport, probably because I was taller than most. But I suffered from all the jumping and landing, and dislocated the patella in both knees fairly often, which was extremely painful, and probably led to my bad knees in later life.

My first introduction to French had been through a very sweet relative when I was still very young: Auntie Louie, who was the second wife of my great-uncle George Anderson, a very well-educated gentleman who was a doctor in London. He had studied medicine at Galway University, reputedly walking many miles to catch the bus to get there. There he met his first wife, Arabella Platt or Aunt Bella, who was, according to my family lore, the daughter of Galway University's provost. She died in 1949 and he married Rachel Louise Perry in London in 1951, so I must have been about six when I met her. I remember her labelling all the household items with French names.

On the curriculum at Ashleigh, as at all grammar schools in those days, French was the main language taught. We had a sweet little lady, whom we called the Mouse as she was very shy, to introduce us to this romantic language. Having been well-grounded in English grammar, we found French grammar quite similar, apart from the masculinity and femininity of the nouns. Though I don't think I ever shone at any language study, we were young enough to quickly absorb the vocabulary and make a passable attempt at speaking it.

When I was about 14, it was suggested I could spend a summer at a Brethren Children's holiday camp in France: Colonie de Vacances at Le Chambon-sur-Lignon, Massif Central. This idea appealed to me greatly, as I longed to see more of the world.

It started with my first aeroplane flight, which took me to Paris in the company of some other young people from Northern Ireland: Stephen and Honor Williamson, my friends Yvonne Allen, Angela McCaw and Sancia Hanna, and my second cousin Lynn Hagan.

After a train journey from the airport to St Etienne, we were met at the station by the director of the Colonie de Vacances in a small Citroen CV. The quirky little car with a push-pull gear change and right-hand drive came as my first foreign surprise. The English director, Edmund Buckenham, known as Oncl' Edmonde at camp, was a terse little man whose attributes we would later discover. Travelling through some spectacular mountain scenery, we arrived at the small market town of Le Chambon-sur-Lignon, which was the nearest town to the camp, further up in the mountains, where we were to stay. The children and helpers were housed in either canvas tents or Swiss-style wooden houses. Here we met Edmund's Northern Irish wife Esther (known as 'Tante Esther'), a happy, buxom lady, whom we would either grow to love or, in some cases, find difficult and disapproving. We also met her two small boys, the French-speaking Algerian cook Tante Rose and the camp nurse, Tante Louise, who was Swiss. Our first meal was of delicious, freshly baked French bread, spread with the most wonderful jam (or 'confiture' as we learned to call it). The bread was totally unlike our Northern Irish sliced loaf, the butter and cheese tasted so different, and the coffee... well! It was nothing like the instant drink made from powder we had thought was coffee. Hot chocolate was another favourite. The term 'culture shock' had not yet been invented, but it described how we felt!

Camping under the tall fir trees in canvas tents was an adventure never to be forgotten. The weather was mild and sunny, and we adapted quickly to this new habitat – apart from the night when I felt a tickle in my pyjamas and discovered an earwig had burrowed its way in and was making its way up my leg. Often we would take long walking trips into the mountains or down to the river, where we would swim and often sunbathe. To me it was a life of bliss, so unlike the Northern Irish culture I had grown up in. Except for the further culture shock of learning to take children's temperatures rectally, and administering drugs the same way.

Activities were planned for the children and, although our French was not very good, we were encouraged to take part and help when we could. After lunch there was always a type of siesta, when the children went to their dorms for a time and Oncl' Edmonde led a period of relaxation therapy, which was something I had never experienced in Northern Ireland. I was a bit dubious at first, as we had been taught at home that these eastern practices were highly suspicious, but I soon came to admire the process and the effect it had on the children, calming them and inducing total relaxation after their energetic play in the morning.

Our main duties, however, were to do with the kitchen. We must have peeled hundreds of potatoes and stripped dozens of artichokes. I still love dipping artichoke leaves in French dressing and sucking out the wonderful juice. Other days we packed picnics of French bread, boiled eggs, and huge beef tomatoes and went up into the mountains. This was where I discovered 'La vache qui rit' – a processed cheese – and the joy of spooning up plain yoghourt topped with granulated sugar. Another delicacy which I got quite addicted to was hazelnut crème, sucked direct from the tube – such bliss. And gradually our French started to improve as we used it with the children and the other workers. And then there was the gorgeous Flavien whose photo I still have, a memory convincing me I had to marry a French man!

What struck me as another anomaly took place on Sundays after church. As it was a Christian camp, run by Brethren missionaries (which was why we were allowed to go there), we visited the local church each Sunday, and it was here that I had yet another culture shock. Yes, we sang the same hymns – in French of course but the tunes were the same and I got to know the French words quite quickly. But coming out of the tiny building, I was amazed to see some of the men lighting up cigarettes. At home, smoking was considered not just a nasty habit but a dreadful sin. (The health aspect was not considered in either place).

We went there for two or three summers. My final trip to camp was in 1962, the year we sat our GCE O-level exams. We had arranged to have our results posted to us at the camp. The day finally arrived, and we nervously opened our big envelopes. What a shock! I had achieved six credits and a pass. I quickly checked the name, as I was sure I had been sent someone else's results by mistake. In my mock finals, my marks had been considerably lower, and in consequence I had been told there was no need for me to return to the sixth form for A-levels, as I would not be clever enough to go to university. So it had been decided that, following the example of several of my aunts, I was to go into a career in nursing....

This is me aged about five

My Dad, Henry Catherwood

My mother, Muriel

Our Sunday School class with teacher Geraldine, best friend Yvonne and myself framing the picture

My brother Arthur and I with the local kids living at Rosetta Parade and Rosetta Drive back in the '50s

Our First Car, a Vauxhall 10, which my father loved!

With Honor Williamson, Angela McCaw, Sancia Hanna and Yvonne Allen at l'Hermon children's camp in France

Wearing the Royal Victoria Hospital 'Fall' and the traditional Staff Nurse uniform

43

At my 21st birthday party at home in Rosetta Parade, Belfast, with nursing friends, Yvonne Allen and two small cousins

2
FIRST LOVE

'Wanted and eventually got: a husband!'

Ever since I was quite small, I had always had a sense that I should someday find a soul-mate, a husband probably. The problem was having been brought up in the Brethren I was expected to marry someone who was also a member. But I knew, early on, that I did NOT want this. The boys in the church never inspired me – though some of the older charismatic preachers did, and so I fantasised a bit about them, often imagining they were looking at me as they preached. Being somewhat shy, I found it hard to chat up boys, even after I started work. And those who did ask me out were never the sort I found attractive. At a visit to my dentist for the free 21st birthday check-up, I was asked 'Have you a boyfriend?' and promptly burst into tears! In my room at night, I pondered the question. I came to the conclusion that I had a lot of love to give, and would just have to hope for the best that I would meet someone I could give it to.

It was 1967, the year that I was taking my final nursing exams at the Royal Victoria Hospital. The three years' training had passed quickly, and I had enjoyed the whole experience. I had gained confidence in myself as an adult and had settled down in a two-bed flat in Broadway Towers, shared with various nursing friends. To me the flat was the essence of modernity – teak units attached to the wall, not the floor; an open-plan kitchen with a breakfast bar; and a shower instead of a bath. It was demanded that once we finished training and passed our exams, we should continue as staff nurses in the hospital for six months, so the future was secure in the short term. My job was in the Metabolic Unit as a staff nurse. At one stage I shared my room with my second cousin Lynn, who had trained as a children's nurse. She tended to be the wild child, whereas I appeared to be quiet and dutiful. Our mothers even arranged a dinner for us with two boys they approved of. The boys were perfectly nice and pleasant company, but sadly for them were not really to our taste.

I soon became friendly with a crowd from the Art College where my best friend from Sunday School, Yvonne, was studying art. I was invited to parties with her, one being in a flat on Rugby Road in the university area, and it was there I first heard The Beatles' LP Sgt Pepper's Lonely Hearts Club Band and discussed fashion and music with this wonderful 'hippy' crowd. One of Yvonne's friends was Gladys, who came from Benburb and whose boyfriend John was also an art student. In autumn 1967 I was invited to Gladys's 21st birthday party 'up the country', and it was arranged we would share lifts, meeting at the car park at Shaw's Bridge on the outskirts of Belfast. I duly arrived and met up with some friends there. The party invitation stated that we should wear something Irish or green and decorate our faces with flowers, 60s style. I had a short green miniskirt I felt would be just right, and had decorated my face with painted floral designs. The anticipation was great. I had just turned 21.

Requiring a lift in a car, I found myself in the back seat with a very cool, bespectacled young man called Christopher Dennis Brown. Like me, he was wearing an Aran sweater. We started to get to know each other on the journey. And somehow that night my life took on a new course.

I sensed that I had met someone who was right on my wavelength. Chris's parents, it turned out, were part of the local evangelical Christian scene, and even had some connections with the Brethren, the denomination my family attended. But there was a freshness in Chris's attitude to life that I felt myself warming to. And the party was a real hit! The venue was a barn, and we were taxied up the hill to the cottage by tractor and trailer. We sat on bales of hay, with music coming from an old gramophone by an open fire, and the food was Irish stew. Before long Chris and I were kissing on a hay bale, until suddenly I noticed everyone was looking at us. But I didn't care! I had met the love of my life. It was love at first sight, and as we chatted I realised we had many things in common.

I found out lots about Chris as the weeks progressed and we spent time together. His parents had been missionaries in China but had to come home in 1945 as his father was in poor health. Chris was born soon after they returned to Northern Ireland. The church provided them with a house in Holywood, Co Down, and the China Inland Mission found Chris's father another job, first of all as General Secretary of the mission in Northern Ireland and later covering the whole of the UK. This meant he was away travelling quite a lot and the family did not see much of him. It was a big shock to them all when in 1958 he had a severe heart attack while away in Edinburgh, and died there.

After his father died, his mother started teaching at Holywood Primary School. Chris and his brother Terence went to school at Sullivan Upper Preparatory School, and later to the upper school, where they both did well. After this Terence went on to Trinity College, Dublin, where he was to become professor of Anglo-Irish Literature, and Chris to Queen's University in Belfast to study

Economics. At university, Chris joined the International Student Movement and spent a good deal of his summer vacations travelling in the Netherlands and Scandinavia – Amsterdam and East Norway in 1964, Copenhagen in 1965, Sweden and Finland in 1966. Recently he had been on a trip to Norway in a small Mini with his friend Paul Bromley, who I also knew as he went to the Brethren assembly we belonged to.

After graduating from Queen's in June 1967, Chris went on to train in hospital administration, and was working in the Royal Victoria Hospital in Belfast when we met. Later he was to move on to the Civil Service to study health service management. While there he wrote a paper on attitudes to cancer in Northern Ireland, and another on cervical cytology.

Chris and I discovered we were at a similar stage in our religious outlook: we had duly surrendered to our faith in our teens, but were now starting to question ideas we had been taught in church and at home. We were on a journey of faith together that had a long way to go. Chris told me his grandfather had been Brethren but had been thrown out as he had disagreed with them about the inspiration of the Bible. I was greatly intrigued by this as I had questions of my own on this subject.

Chris asked me to marry him about six weeks after we met. But my mother seemed to go into shock as it had all happened so quickly. So my parents thought we should wait for a year before getting married. While we were engaged, we had a wonderful time in spite of my parents' caution. We went out together to the cinema and shows. I met Chris's mother and brother, and had wonderful meals at their house, where the conversation seemed much more stimulating than at home. I started attending Berry Street Presbyterian Church where his family belonged, and loved sitting beside this gorgeous new man I had found.

48

Chris was the one outstanding best thing that ever happened to me. It had been love at first sight, and I had not a doubt that he was the one for me. I was a shy, awkward, mixed-up product of a Brethren upbringing, and by loving and accepting me, and seeing potential in me, he transformed me into a very different, independent and more stable person.

1968: Our Engagement

My parents had insisted we wait for a year before getting married. However, this time was not wasted, as I had arranged to go to London to train as a midwife, and coincidentally Chris was sent on a course in personnel management, which also took place in London and later Manchester. We had a wonderful time exploring the capital. We were very much in love, and to avoid accidents I saw a family planning doctor about going on the pill. My mother would have been very annoyed had she known, but would have been even more upset if I had gotten pregnant, which was her worst nightmare.

My hospital, Queen Charlotte's Maternity Hospital in Chiswick, provided free tickets to shows and restaurants in London. It was the Swinging Sixties, and we had a ball! I shared a flat in Chiswick with other nurses, and we would all set off to the West End with our free tickets. We ate Hungarian goulash in basement restaurants, and went to BBC shows such as Harry Worth and the Black and White Minstrels. While Chris was up in Manchester I would take a train there for the weekend, and enjoyed a party life I had never experienced before. For the first time ever, I even pulled a sickie in order to stay longer in Manchester.

Chris bought himself a blue second-hand Triumph Herald convertible, and we drove to Bristol and the West Country to meet his aunt and cousins who lived there. We started making plans for our wedding, and I was the happiest girl in the world! But Chris's course in London was for a shorter time than mine, and he then had to go back to Northern Ireland to continue training. His next placement was at St Luke's Hospital in Armagh, and from there he wrote me wonderful love letters which I still have and treasure. We missed each other a lot.

I decided that midwifery was not for me. I completed Part 1 of the midwifery course but decided to go back to Northern Ireland in early 1969 to arrange the details of the Big Day in April. My mother's sister Myra, who lived in London with her hotelier husband Bernie, had met us a few times while we were there. She expressed her deep concern that my mother would not be able to cope with a big wedding. She advised us to go and get married quietly, but we would have none of it. We wanted our friends to share in our joy. Sadly, I later found out Aunt Myra had been right about my mother.

1969: Our wedding

By then, as it was over a year since we had become engaged, a date was set for the wedding: 9th April 1969. Preparations got underway. However, as the day drew close, my mother started to become very tense about the whole process. For my part, I knew Chris was the answer to my dreams. But to my mother, it was just a flight of fancy. In her mind, she had conjured up ideas of unwanted pregnancy, emotional break-ups, even losing her daughter. 'You should wait a year,' she said, and to keep her happy we complied. It was as if my mother had never envisaged her only daughter marrying and leaving home. Her mind was tortured with the thought of life not following the path she expected it to. If someone in the family died, she fell apart. If someone left the confines of their family and went abroad, even made a success of their life, she was in tears.

So Chris and I had had a long engagement; at least it seemed long to us. Now, as our big day approached, tension increased in our house. The 'At Home' evenings, with displays of wedding presents, tray bakes and best frocks became a threat: was the room well-enough decorated; was there enough food; why did Mrs B not attend? I spent more time with my fiancé than with my family. Nothing would hinder the process of marrying the man of my dreams.

The day arrived. Aunts and friends helped me prepare for the ceremony. My mother was in tears, unable to leave her bed. An aunt tried to help her get into the outfit she had chosen. Eventually they asked me to help her to get out of bed. But no, the demons had taken over. Yet I was strangely calm, as it became apparent that my mother would not be present at the church.

I knew my father must have been distressed by the turn of events, but he alone was there for me as the limousine arrived at the front door. It was a windy April day, and we set off to the church together, leaving an aunt to stay with my mother until the doctor arrived and recommended she be admitted to a local hospital.

In Northern Ireland terms, this was a 'mixed marriage'. We had decided to have the service in my Brethren church with the Presbyterian minister from Chris's church officiating, as he was a recognised registrar of marriages and the Brethren preacher was not. As Chris's Aunt Irene had a dress shop in Belfast, 'Renee Meneely's', I was given as a wedding present one of the fabulous dresses there. It was quite a windy day, and as I was getting out of the wedding car, the wind blew my beautiful long veil over my face. My bridesmaids Yvonne (my old Sunday School friend) and Lynn, my second cousin, joined my father and me as we entered the classical Victorian building, which had once been a music hall. Together we climbed the curved sweeping steps to the upper hall where the ceremony was to take place. I was sad for my mother but stuck to my plans without regret, knowing for sure this marriage was right for me.

The wedding reception followed at the Culloden Hotel near Holywood with friends and family. Chris made an impromptu speech from his notes, literally on the back of an envelope. Photos were taken in the sweeping grounds of the hotel, and I changed from my beautiful dress into a navy-blue 'going-away' outfit with a pillbox hat, also from Renee Meneely's dress shop. Unlike today's couples who sensibly take a night at home before going on honeymoon, we then took a taxi to the airport and a flight to London, where we were to be treated to a night in the Piccadilly Hotel by my Aunt Myra, whose husband Bernie was currently the CEO of Grand Metropolitan Hotels. Next day we were to fly off for a holiday in Tunisia.

But although I was not aware of it, things had already started to go wrong early that morning. My husband-to-be had appeared rather difficult to rouse, and had complained of feeling a little groggy. Which may not have seemed surprising, considering the stag party of the night before. However, it was the Big Day and he had managed to crawl out of bed and squeeze into his tails and pin stripes. At the ceremony, everything had appeared to be progressing fine. We had been duly married and whisked off to the reception. The photographs were a bit tedious, and Chris especially seemed relieved when the standing was over. At the meal his appetite was poor, but this could have been due to any number of things – excitement, last-minute immunisations, indigestion from the night before... Or, as his mother cheerfully suspected, perhaps a threatening appendix?

As our plane took off for London, my newly married husband complained of stomach ache. Nerves, I thought, and gave him a painkiller. He was no better on arrival at the hotel, but we tried to settle down in the wonderful hotel grandeur of the Piccadilly. Just asleep, we wakened to a dripping sound. Water was soaking the foot of the bed! Reception traced the problem to an overflowing bath in the room above. They promised to move us to a vacant room, but none were available. Finally we were allocated the manager's penthouse suite on the top floor! Cases were repacked at 2am and moved to the penthouse suite, and we tried to enjoy this unexpected luxury.

But alas, no sex tonight, Josephine! By 3am, a doctor had to be called. He charged us exorbitantly for a ten minute consultation, and diagnosed appendicitis. Chris was sent by ambulance to the Middlesex Hospital, where he joined the victims of Soho stabbings and drug overdoses in casualty. I followed by tube train, glad of the anonymity of London as the tears flowed down my face and the other passengers looked away. At the Middlesex, there were sad jokes: 'Sorry, we can't provide double beds, ho-ho-ho!'

Sorrowfully, I called my aunt Myra, who had supplied the hotel room, and she sensibly arranged to meet me for dinner in a nearby restaurant. Schooners of sherry appeared, followed by champagne. 'It's your wedding night!' she proclaimed, and I had to agree, though all I could think about was that Chris was not here to enjoy it. All I wanted was to get back to see him. Eventually we left the restaurant, and I stumbled down the steep spiral staircase, realising the champagne had gone to my head. I worried what the nurses would think: this poor man's wife getting drunk while he was operated on!

At the hospital we were ushered towards the ward he had been in. The bed was empty and re-made. 'Oh no, he's died!' I thought, 'and I've just been out drinking!' Happily, he had just been moved to another spot in the ward, and was fuzzily resurfacing from his anaesthetic.

While Chris recovered, I moved into my old flat in London, which I had just vacated and which now had empty beds, as some of my flatmates had gone to Belfast for our wedding. The others blinked, unbelieving: 'You're supposed to be on honeymoon!'

Chris soon recovered, but was impatient to be out of the hospital. Eventually he signed himself out, and my aunt arranged for another few nights in the hotel while he gathered the strength to return home. We tried to enjoy the few days left of our honeymoon, but Chris soon became exhausted. We walked around Piccadilly, then to the Design Centre, which we had been keen to see, but his legs gave way there and he collapsed onto one of the beautiful designer chairs that we were considering buying for our new home. When holiday insurance eventually paid up for our cancelled trip to Tunisia, we spent the money on furniture.

So we had an eventful start to our married life. Little did we know what was to follow in the years to come. This song by the Kinks, written by Raymond Douglas Davies, says how I feel about him now:

> *Thank you for the days, those endless days, those sacred days you   gave   me.*
> *I'm thinking of the days. I won't forget a single day, believe me.*
> *I bless the light, I bless the light that shines on you, believe me,*
> *And though you're gone, you're with me every single day, believe   me.*
> *Days I'll remember all my life; days when you can't see wrong   from   right,*
> *You took my life, and then I knew that very soon you'd leave*

me.

But it's all right, now I'm not frightened of this world, believe
me.

I	*wish*	*today*	*could*	*be*	*tomorrow.*
The		*night*		*is*	*dark,*
It	*just*	*brings*		*sorrow*	*anyway.*

Thank you for the days…

Intervening Years

There followed 14 happy years of marriage. Our three children arrived – Jenny in 1972, Niall in 1976 and Jonathan in 1981.

Our first home was a rented flat in Belfast, then a tiny bungalow in Dundonald, bought for £3,000. Next we moved to a new-build out in the country at Ballinree Park, Killinchy, Co Down in 1973. I didn't take to this house and we only stayed 18 months. However, the market was on our side when we sold it, and the price enabled us to get a four-bed house: 1 Tudor Oaks in Holywood.

Highlights of our married life before the children came along included a summer school in Oxford in 1970, where we hired a houseboat on the river, and a romantic trip to Paris the same year. The following year we holidayed in Arklow, Co Wicklow. And around 1973 I joined the Killinchy Singers.

In 1973, Chris and his friend Richard set up a business venture in our house at Killinchy making hot-water cylinder jackets, or 'Killinchy Mufflers' as they called their new product. According to the BBC Ulster Scots page, a Killinchy Muffler is 'someone's arm around your neck, or a cuddle' and it was the local phrase for 'a big warm cuddle'. (No other explanation for the phrase seems to be available. Were people who lived in Killinchy especially loving? Or is it connected with the cold breezes from Strangford Lough?) Anyway, it was the time when the cost of oil and heating products were just beginning to rise, and my husband Chris, being an entrepreneur-in-the-making, saw a niche market with the possibility of starting a business in insulation products. The Killinchy Muffler was his first idea, followed closely by polystyrene granules. He and Richard rented premises and proceeded to experiment at home with methods to blow granules from A to B. This involved putting our home vacuum cleaner into reverse, and for months I was finding small white pebbles, light as air, in the corners of every room and indeed in many other spaces and orifices, both household and personal, also in the garden and probably outer space. Richard was a fun person, scruffy but observant and interested in everything around him. Unfortunately, he had a drink problem, and soon Chris had to find another business partner. Strangford Insulation Products was then set up in Newtownards with a new partner in 1975.

1977, according to my diary, was quite eventful. It was the year Jenny started primary school, and she and Niall promptly caught measles. We started building an extension and new kitchen at our house; the new kitchen was forced on us due to a fire. In July Chris moved his factory to new premises. We settled down to a busy suburban life: ballet and Brownies for Jenny; business management for Chris; church fellowship and child care for me. In 1978, Auntie Myra died and I went to London for her funeral at Westminster Chapel. Her husband gave me her pearls, which had belonged to his French-Russian grandmother. We took family holidays in Scotland and Portugal, and in 1980 Chris and I treated ourselves to a few days in Copenhagen, leaving my parents to look after eight-year-old Jenny and four-year-old Niall. With the arrival of Jonathan, I started marking off the milestones of infancy in my diary: nappy rash, wakeful nights, teething, crawling, chicken pox … Jenny brought the school guinea pig home for the holidays and Chris took Niall to the Transport Museum for his birthday treat.

But our happy family life was to suddenly fall apart...

Shadows Gather

Most people, I expect, at some time spend a sleepless night imagining that they or their partner might have some dreaded disease; there may be a queried X-ray, a strange lump, a spot of blood on a handkerchief, and the fact of our mortality dawns suddenly upon us. Happily, the worry usually turns out to be groundless. But occasionally the vague fear will turn into a leaden feeling in the pit of the stomach, when the normally reassuring clerk on the phone refuses to be committed, and talks strangely about further tests. Such was my experience when it was suspected that my husband Chris had leukaemia.

The winter of 1982 was unusually severe, bringing with it flu viruses which many people found hard to shake off. Chris was no exception, and his flu was followed by earache and then a tooth abscess. These left him feeling very tired, but he carried on with work as usual, though strangely it seemed he was finding it hard to relax completely in the evenings as he usually did.

One evening, Chris was feeling particularly tense, although he seemed to have recovered at last from the flu. I had been wondering if some relaxation therapy might help, and decided to try this at home first, and if possible discover the cause of this tension. As I massaged, there seemed to be a hardness in his abdominal muscles, which no amount of massage would relieve. It seemed to be more on the left side, which led me to suspect, being a nurse, that perhaps it was a tumour in the stomach area. I was horrified, but said nothing then, and instead spoke to a medical friend, who of course said Chris should see his GP. This he did, and the doctor was reassuring, suggesting it might be a muscle injury. He asked if Chris had been involved in any street violence, or a rugby match. He had been in neither, but somehow I wanted to cling to that small glimmer of hope.

An appointment was made with a surgeon. We went privately to reduce any waiting time, as by now Chris was getting worried. He saw the surgeon on a Thursday, and had blood and other tests taken. On the Friday morning the hospital phoned me to ask if Chris could come in for further tests. I sensed of course that something was indeed badly wrong, but the voice on the phone refused to give any further information, leaving me to imagine the worst. That weekend was to Chris the worst time of the whole illness – suspecting, but not knowing. On the Thursday, when he had seen the surgeon, he had been told that his spleen was enlarged. This explained the swelling on his left side. For Chris, the next logical step was to look up my nursing textbooks while I was out. From these he realised it had to be one of three things: malaria, cirrhosis of the liver or leukaemia. Sunday was dreadful, as we could do nothing except mull it over. We had some guests in the evening, which of course did not really take our minds off the nightmare at all.

On the Monday morning, Chris went into Ards Hospital. Blood tests confirmed that the white cells were greatly increased, and it was decided to do a biopsy of the bone marrow where the white cells are formed. Chris was able to phone and tell me this himself. His words confirmed my worst fears. From my nursing training I knew it must be leukaemia.

Most of that day was spent in tears. A close friend looked after Jonathan, our youngest, then aged nine months, while I went to the hospital. Chris and I saw the haematologist together and were told officially what we already knew.

It seemed that our normal if somewhat humdrum existence had suddenly come to a standstill. The future stretched ahead uncertain, but I instinctively felt the need to reach out to God, realising somehow that from now on we would have to experience a much greater dependence on Him. And how true that was to be. The doctor had given us a fairly hopeful prognosis with the use of the latest drugs, but was honest enough to tell us that Chris's life span would probably be shortened. Chris made it clear from the start that he wanted to know all the facts, and from that day when he was told the diagnosis he was much more content in himself. But in that hospital room we just clung together, weeping unashamedly. He kept asking how I would cope, and I kept reassuring him that I would manage, as I always did in a crisis. Inwardly I was less sure and was wondering just how it would affect me.

A course of drugs was commenced that day to reduce the number of white blood cells. I left the hospital in a daze, meeting strangers on the stairs and wondering how they could act so normally – but of course they did not know my world was falling apart. Driving home on my own, blinded by tears but asking God for His help, I had only one positive thought: that Chris would have the joy of seeing Him before I would. All else seemed bleak – the children fatherless, the one I loved no longer there. How could I ever cope? Physically, I knew I could handle the everyday running of the family and the house, but emotionally and psychologically Chris was my mainstay and the only person with whom I could feel totally relaxed and at ease, and to whom I could open my heart completely. It was devastating.

In a few days Chris was home. He first phoned our minister, Rev John Ross, who was shattered by the news and came round immediately. We found him as great a help then as he was to prove to be in the future. Next, Chris saw our solicitor, who proceeded to be very practical and positive about the whole situation. The next few days and weeks drew Chris and I very close together, as we realised how precious every day would be to us from then on.

The summer after Chris was diagnosed was a difficult one. In previous years, before his diagnosis, we had holidayed in Paris; Oxford; Rathlin Island; a caravan in Newcastle, Co Down; Portnoo, Donegal; Arklow, Co Wicklow; Portnablagh, Donegal; Ballycastle; Scotland; Rossnowlagh, Donegal; Portugal; Copenhagen; and Killoskehane Castle, Co Tipperary. While he was in remission, we checked with the doctor if a holiday in Lanzarote would be possible, and he agreed. We flew out of Dublin in the spring, with the snow still on the ground, looking forward to some precious family time together, and I was inwardly hoping and praying there would be no health problems.

Unfortunately, soon after arriving, I developed a tummy bug. This cleared up in a day or so, and we enjoyed the rest of the time, mostly by the hotel pool with the children. But just before we left, Chris caught the bug and was quite sick. On the plane I kept asking for water for him, but the plane was crowded and the attendants were busy, though I think we did get it in the end. Arriving at Dublin Airport, we found the car covered in snow, and had an hour-long drive in front of us to Holywood in the north of Ireland. Jonathan was still being breast fed so, even though Chris was feeling really ill, I had to share the driving with him when the baby needed attention. On the journey Chris developed a severe pain in his chest, and I was worried it might be something serious. Each time we saw a sign for a hospital we considered stopping, but felt it would probably be better to get back home and call our own doctor. We arrived back in the small hours and called the surgery, but there was some problem with getting referred to the out-of-hours service and eventually we phoned our doctor friend Ian, who was a geriatric consultant but was well-aware of Chris's problems. He admitted Chris to hospital immediately, where he was told he had pleurisy.

The Nightmare is Real

I remember asking Chris at this stage if his faith was a help to him, and he replied that maybe the illness had helped his faith. In the past he had not often talked about his personal faith in God, but now I sensed that he was beginning to reach out more in faith, and was indeed finding the help he so desperately needed. All through his illness we would read the Psalms together and other helpful Christian books, and he seemed to draw strength from them.

STRENGTH – that was something I knew I would need in the months to come. Not just physical strength, but the deep underlying spiritual strength that only God could give. The verse I clung to then was Psalm 73 v.26: 'But God is the strength of my heart.' I felt that spiritual strength was important, and would help me rise above whatever problems might present themselves. I sometimes used an old-fashioned prayer by Annie Johnson Flint:

Give me Thy strength for Thy day, Lord, that wheresoe'er I go,
There shall no danger daunt me, and I shall fear no foe;
So shall no task o'ercome me; so shall no trial fret;
So shall I walk unwearied the path where my feet are set;
So shall I find no burden greater than I can bear;
So shall I have a courage equal to all my care;
So shall no grief o'erwhelm me;
So shall no wave o'erflow;

> *Give me Thy strength for my day, Lord.*
> *Cover my weakness so.*

At this stage also, many thoughts were beginning to go through my mind, sometimes confusing, sometimes stretching me in my Christian understanding...

Was all this a kind of test in order to make us better Christians? John 15 v.2 states: 'Every branch that does bear fruit, He prunes, that it may bring forth more fruit.'

Should we be confidently going out on a limb to ask God to miraculously heal Chris? John 15 v.7 reads 'If you abide in me, and my words abide in you, ask whatever you will and it shall be done for you.'

Job 23 v.3-11 was a comfort and an encouragement: '....I cannot see Him; but he knoweth the way that I take: when he hath tried me, I shall come forth as gold. My foot hath held his steps, His way have I kept.' I wanted to do God's will, to come forth as gold from the furnace. In my head I knew I could trust Him, but that meant that I must relinquish Chris to Him in my heart. I did, in fact, reach a point where I believed I had relinquished him to God in faith, only to discover much later, in a crisis, that I had not.

The next few weeks were spent trying to get used to the fact that our whole world had been turned upside down. For us both it meant a lot of soul searching about what had happened. For Chris it meant finding out everything about leukaemia and its treatment. He was fascinated by it in a very subjective way. The treatment had a scientific approach that appealed to his mind, more than the cruder treatments of some other sorts of cancer might have done. The disease itself produced little actual discomfort, and once on treatment he felt his strength gradually returning. The drugs themselves produced some side-effects: nausea and some referred pain in the left shoulder, caused as his spleen reduced in size. Chris coped well with these, and kept up a cheerful image, though there were times when he did feel down – he loved life and really did not want to let go of it just yet. He was back at work, though he sometimes came home at midday if the pain or nausea was bothering him.

At first, only a few close friends knew of his illness, and their support at that time was invaluable. My initial reaction, strangely, had been to let as few people as possible know of his illness. I had a horror of people nudging each other in the supermarket and saying pityingly, 'That poor girl's husband has leukaemia.' I suppose it was my mind's subconscious way of giving me time to adjust to the news myself before breaking it to others. However, Chris and I knew we would soon have to break the news to our families. How do you ever start to tell the members of a family that one of their nearest and dearest has an incurable disease? I tried to explain in simple terms to the children what was happening to their Daddy. About two weeks after the diagnosis, Chris was beginning to feel quite positive and optimistic about his prognosis. He had great faith in modern medicine and believed that God could work through that medium. Courageously he spoke to each member of his family himself, giving the facts, but allowing his hope to shine out. For his mother, it took some time for the underlying seriousness of the condition to sink in, but this also served to soften the blow for her. His brother Terence and sister-in-law Sue were deeply shocked, but Terence immediately offered his bone marrow for transplant if necessary.

Gradually, the rest of our friends heard the news, and their reactions varied from, 'Trust you to get something out of the ordinary!' to obviously being deeply upset. People who had known Chris many years beforehand eventually got to find out and came to call. Sometimes they stayed too long and tired him out.

Our church continued to be increasingly supportive, both in prayer and in practical ways. I had one difficult evening at choir practice, when we were singing 'Be still, my soul' and I couldn't bear to sing the words about 'dearest friends departing'. I fled in tears to the cloakroom, where I was found and comforted by a good friend. Going to church was helpful but sometimes emotional, especially if Chris was prayed for in public. Many people found it difficult to know what to say, and we often found it was up to us to put people at their ease, rather than the other way around.

Peaks and Valleys

The possibility of healing was something we had thought about a lot and discussed with various people. Some thought that the elders of the church should be called, in accordance with James 4 v.14-16, and Chris tended to agree with this. I was keen for him to go to someone who had a definite gift of healing, and some supported me on this, though we had no one in particular in mind. We were in agreement though that if Chris were to be healed, it must surely bring glory to God, and our faith would be vindicated.

However, before we had come to any decision, a person visited our church who was thought to have been greatly used by God in the field of divine healing. His name was Derek Prince. Although Chris had at one time been somewhat sceptical of this sort of thing, he went along with an open mind. Derek Prince seemed to specialise mainly in back problems, but Chris was so impressed with the whole service that he decided to take the opportunity to go forward and ask for healing. Many people we knew had already done so, and had experienced healing before our very eyes.

Dr Prince spoke to Chris for a few minutes. Chris said afterwards that when he touched him, he felt a power surge through him, followed by a sense of spiritual uplift. Then he passed out on the floor for a few minutes. I was sitting on my own at this stage, and suddenly felt overcome with emotion and burst into tears. A friend who had just been healed of a back problem came and sat beside me. It was seeing her face so full of joy as she was healed that had prompted Chris to take the first step to the front.

Chris felt fine afterwards. His next blood test was due in about 10 days. The result of this test was completely normal for the first time since the start of his illness. We were of course overjoyed. The haematologist admitted that the disease was in remission, but insisted that this was due to the drugs. When told of the healing service, his reply was, 'We can do with all the help we can get!' Chris's drugs were drastically reduced, and I was keen for him to ask for further tests to be done immediately to show that he was indeed healed, as I sometimes believed he was. Chris seemed strangely unconcerned, and would not ask the doctor to do this.

On discussing it all with Chris I found out something very vital concerning his faith. We knew that he had had a spiritual experience that night at the healing service. But whereas Derek Prince and I had perhaps limited our faith to praying for the healing of the disease, Chris himself had found faith to believe that whatever happened, his life was in God's hands, that God was in control, and that all would be for the best. His own attitude to healing was that although Jesus had healed many people, not one of them was still alive, so in fact all physical healing is only temporary. Spiritual healing, however, such as Chris experienced, is forever. From that time on, he had a wonderful peace inside him, and a radiance that was commented upon by anyone who met him. He put out of his mind the possibilities and impossibilities of the situation, and got on with living, trusting quietly in God. That trust has been a help to me, and still is as I face the future without Chris, but with the knowledge that God is in control.

Chris was very well all summer, and we had a lovely week together as a family in Donegal. After the holiday he went back to work, and gradually got more involved in it again. His brother Terence and family came to visit at the end of August. Terence had his blood checked for compatibility for a bone marrow transplant, which was beginning to seem a viable proposition and in fact a possible cure.

That weekend, Chris had an earache, which was treated with antibiotics, but on the Monday evening he felt tired and went to bed with a slightly raised temperature. All that week his temperature continued to rise and fall, and he lost his appetite and felt very weak. We called the doctor, who asked the haematologist to come and see him. After some tests, the haematology specialist confided to me that the leukaemia could be going into an acute phase, and arranged for Chris to go into hospital the next day. I found this very upsetting, and with Chris's agreement phoned John Ross and asked if he would come to the house with some of the elders to pray for Chris, as I was so concerned about his condition.

That evening, John Ross and four others came to the house, and first of all spent some time downstairs praying with me. They read Psalm 46, which commences: 'God is our refuge and strength, a very present help in time of trouble. Therefore we will not fear, though the earth should change, though the mountains shake in the heart of the sea.' I found this hard to accept, or even to contemplate that the worst might happen. I would have preferred a psalm of triumphant or even defiant hope, such as Psalm 30, which Chris and I had read often from the Living Bible, especially Verse 3: 'You brought me back from the brink of the grave, from death itself, and here I am alive.' Upstairs, we all knelt around the bed, and read again Psalm

46, then oil was poured on Chris's head, and we prayed for him and for whatever the future might hold. I was convinced at this stage that if we believed enough, Chris would be healed, and I felt we did believe enough.

Next day, Chris was admitted to hospital, and as his temperature continued to rise he was given cold compresses, a fan and intravenous antibiotics. A sample of bone marrow was taken again, and to me the result of this test was crucial, as I still felt sure it would prove to be negative. However, when it came through, I was told that the leukaemia was in transformation, i.e. changing to a more acute form. But they said this form was in fact treatable, whereas another form it might otherwise have taken had a prognosis of only nine to 10 weeks.

Only one thing was plain to me as I viewed this turn of events: the tests were not clear, and Chris was still obviously very ill. I went through a very rebellious time then for about a week, feeling that God must be cruel and sadistic to allow this to happen, despite all our prayers and very real faith. (C. S. Lewis also considered the idea of God as 'the Cosmic Sadist' in his book, A Grief Observed.) Why did He not miraculously intervene? Would it not have brought glory to His name? That evening, our elder Ian Taylor called at the house, and I was able to voice my thoughts and feelings to him.

The next day, I made a decision that all this crying and wondering and trying to make sense of things was doing nobody any good. I found that if I stopped thinking about the possibilities, I could just bottle up my emotions and stop hurting. So when John Ross and Roy Millar, another elder, came that evening, I put up a hard front, sitting up straight on the other side of the room, allowing no one to get beneath the surface. I am sure most ministers or church elders would have decided I didn't want to talk and would have left me alone at that stage, but John and Roy that night were guided to gently probe my mind, until finally I broke down and was able to tell them all I felt. How could God cruelly take apart a happy marriage which He himself had created, making us one flesh, yet now break us apart? We talked a lot, but I was on an emotional seesaw, one minute believing Chris would be healed, the next that he would die.

I awoke most nights that week and wept for long periods in the night, often praying from the depths of my being for Chris's healing. One night, at 4am, I wrote a letter to Chris, expressing my feelings. I gave it to him the next day, as I couldn't have said some of those things without breaking down, and I was determined to keep up a happy front when I visited him. I know he treasured that letter for the rest of his days, and I sometimes caught him reading it again at hospital.

There was a 24-hour prayer vigil for Chris in the church at the end of that week. Betty Hewitt, a good friend of ours, told me later that about that time she had been reading in 2nd Kings, and came to the part in Chapter 20 where King Hezekiah became sick and was at the point of death. Isaiah the prophet then told him that the Lord had said that he was going to die, so Hezekiah prayed for healing, and the Lord granted him 15 more years to his life. Betty was saddened as she felt that the Lord was telling her that Chris would indeed be healed, but only for a time. How true this turned out to be. He was starting to respond to the treatment by the following weekend, and when Ian Taylor and I visited him on the Sunday, I was feeling more optimistic. However, certain things Ian said made me feel he was preparing me for the worst. He was talking about how to prepare the children, and mentioned a book by a doctor dying of cancer, entitled Dying, the Greatest Adventure of my Life. I read the book that night and found it helpful, as did my mother who was staying with us. I had felt all along that Chris had achieved a balance between knowing the facts and having faith, and I was just beginning to move towards that state myself, with the help of that book and things that Ian and Roy had said. Being medical doctors as well as church elders, they were well-placed to advise me.

I had been feeling that God was cruel to allow this to happen, and now I was being shown that, as the rain falls on Christians and non-Christians alike, so does suffering. In fact, if being a Christian guaranteed freedom from suffering, people might be jumping on the bandwagon for all the wrong reasons. 'The good man does not escape all troubles – he has them too. But the Lord helps him in each and every one' (Psalm 34 v.19).

I had been angry with God for not using His power to intervene miraculously to heal Chris, and now I was learning that there will be no end to suffering in the world until Christ comes back to reign.

It had seemed to me that God was perhaps using the end to justify the means, i.e. the 'end' of making us better Christians ('I will refine you and you shall come forth as gold') to justify the 'means' of Chris's prolonged illness and possible death. At last I saw that the suffering was not caused by God, but that, if I allowed Him, He could use what Satan had planned for an evil purpose to achieve a greater end, and in this Satan himself would be defeated. 'Do not rejoice against me, O my enemy, for though I fall, I will rise again!' (Micah 7 v.8). This was something I had previously believed in theory only, but knowing it in practice had brought me a stage further in knowing God and understanding His ways.

I read Isaiah 53 v.4 now with new understanding. My grief and sorrow were part of the grief that He bore and the sorrows that He carried, that we might have peace. Because He loved us so much, He took that grief upon himself, and actually felt the pain and the suffering. What was I doing, going through it all again, when all I had to do was to claim His peace, even in the midst of my own trouble? My prayers began to be more positive. I remembered a book

I had read in the summer called Power in Praise, and I praised Him for suffering for me and Chris.

There was one more step I knew I had to take, and that was of relinquishing Chris completely to God. I had definitely prayed at the beginning of Chris's illness that I would be willing to relinquish Chris, if God so willed, but it had become evident to me, now that the time had come when I thought Chris would die, that I hadn't really meant it at all. I just didn't want to accept that God's will might mean his death. Somehow, that weekend, on my own with God, I began to trust Chris to Him, believing that whatever happened could only be for the best in God's reckoning. And so, through praise and trust, I began to receive that peace which passes all understanding, which Chris had learned long before me.

> 'Lord, when doubts fill my mind, when my heart is in turmoil, quiet me and give me renewed hope and cheer.' Psalm 34 v 19.
> 'I thought about the wrong direction in which I was headed, and turned around and came running back to you.' Psalm 119 vs 59 and 60.

Chris continued to improve from that weekend on, and was allowed home sooner, in fact, than we had expected. His appetite was almost insatiable and his strength was returning. I felt that here at last was our answer to prayer and that, despite all the medical statistics, Chris was getting better. I believed at that stage that before I was allowed to see an improvement in Chris's condition it had been necessary for me to go through all that doubting to reach a point of real faith and trust, and from there to offer my sacrifice of praise. I

70

did not know it then, but it was only to be a means of preparing me for what was finally to come.

However, for four weeks Chris was in top form, and enjoying going for walks and doing jobs in the house. His treatment seemed to be working well, although there was still the possibility of doing a bone marrow transplant, which might affect a more lasting cure.

I personally found two songs particularly helpful at that time, and used them to express my gratitude to God. The first was based on Psalm 16, and incidentally was also a help to Canon David Watson, after he knew he had cancer.

'For You are my God, you alone are my joy. Defend me, O Lord.

You give wonderful brothers to me – the faithful who dwell in your land.
Those who chose alien gods have chosen an alien band.
You are my portion and cup. It is you that I claim for my prize.
Your heritage is my delight – the lot you have given to me.
Glad are my heart and my soul! Securely my body shall rest.
For you will not leave me for dead, nor lead your beloved astray.
You show me the path for my life. In your presence is fullness of joy!
To be at your right hand for ever for me would be happiness always!'

'My	*glory*	*and*	*the*	*lifter*	*of*	*my*	*head!*
My	*glory*	*and*	*the*	*lifter*	*of*	*my*	*head!*
O	*thou,*	*O*	*Lord,*	*art a*	*shield*	*to*	*me.*
My	*glory*	*and*	*the*	*lifter*	*of*	*my*	*head!*
I	*cried*	*unto*	*the*	*Lord*	*with*	*my*	*voice.*
I	*cried*	*unto*	*the*	*Lord*	*with*	*my*	*voice.*
I	*cried*	*unto*	*the*	*Lord*	*with*	*my*	*voice.*

And He heard me, out of His holy hill.'

We enjoyed those four weeks together, and they are very precious to me now. We talked about God's goodness, and enjoyed going to church together again. I even re-joined the church choir for the harvest activities, and felt life was becoming more normal again. People in the church were extremely kind to us; they often asked us out for meals and helped with grass-cutting and other heavy jobs. We were, in fact, living on such a 'high' that we never actually talked about the possibility, however remote, of death. We both believed that, whatever happened, God was in control, and all would be for the best in His purposes. I think I refused to think of death at this stage, and just lived for the present, hoping for the future. Chris probably did think about it, but found it too difficult to mention.

Looking back, I can't decide if this was good or bad. On the one hand, not talking about it meant that those four weeks were not clouded in any way. But, practically speaking, it would have been good to check with him exactly where all the life insurance documents were, as some of these were never found. However, this may have been tied up in his mind with business problems, which he never discussed with me either. It was only after he died that I discovered that his business was actually in dire straits financially, and in an uncanny way went into liquidation just about the same time as he died. The business, in fact, died with him. Knowing this, I was amazed in retrospect at his calmness and serenity during those last days. Those who saw him then must agree with me that it was totally illogical.

Graduation photo, Chris Brown

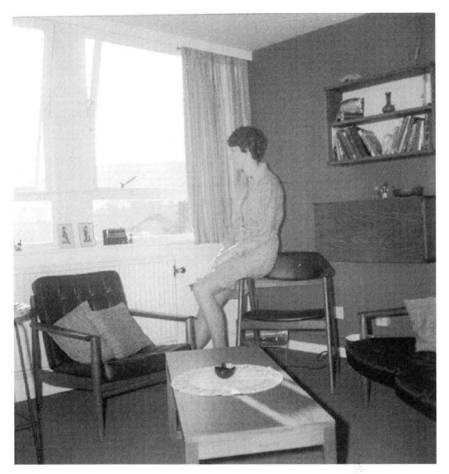

In my flat at Broadway Towers nurses' accommodation at the Royal

Chris and me in his mother's garden in Belfast

With Chris in London, 1968

With bridesmaids Yvonne Allen and Lynn Hagan

Our first home in Dundonald

Chris at our first home in Galway Park, Dundonald

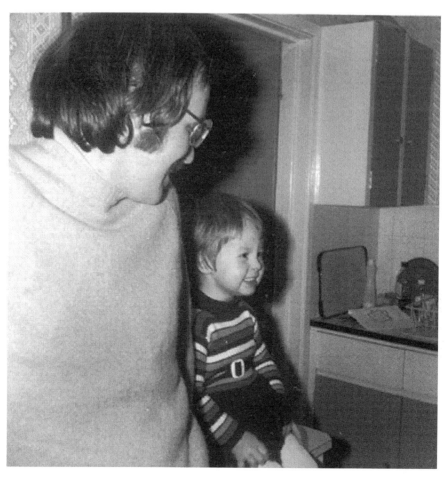

Chris with Jenny at our Killinchy house

3

IT ALL CAME CRASHING DOWN

After those four glorious weeks, on October 10th Chris started feeling tired and his temperature began to rise and fall again. About this time there was more talk of a bone marrow transplant, as Terence's bone marrow was proving to be a good match. On October 14th we had to make the final decision about whether to go ahead with the transplant. Having talked about it together a lot and considered the possibilities, of which Chris was fully aware, our answer was a definite yes. We felt we really had no choice, as another crisis could arise at any time, and the next time he might not survive it at all. The odds were stacked against him, and although he knew the transplant was a very daunting procedure, fraught with risks, he was prepared to go ahead with it because of the hope it held out for him. If it is successful, a bone marrow transplant can in fact be the means to a complete cure. We knew lots of complications could occur immediately following the procedure, but Chris was prepared to accept these risks, along with the inevitable loss of hair and long-term isolation nursing.

I stress again however, the sense of peace he had regarding what would follow, and the fact that he was not as well as he had been only served to convince him that he should have the transplant.

I called the haematologist on Tuesday 19th October, and he came the next day. He told us that the blood tests were now showing signs of change again, and that they would probably go ahead with the transplant fairly soon. Chris was delighted, as he had been worrying that they might leave him for weeks before doing it. He disliked the vagueness of 'fairly soon', but it still came as a big shock when the date was finally set: total radiation on 31st October, and the transplant on 1st November.

There were a lot of preliminary procedures to be set in motion, and a bed was booked for Thursday 21st October, which was in fact the next day. This gave us very little warning, but then the doctor phoned to say they wanted Chris to come in immediately to be ready for the preliminary operation next day.

Thursday morning was rather hectic, with many last-minute phone calls and various visitors, so there was hardly time to think about what was happening. Also, the children were off school for the Assembly elections, and I had to arrange for them to be looked after while I took Chris to hospital. John Ross had arranged to hold a short communion at home with a few elders in the evening, but this had to be changed to lunchtime when the other elders were not free. Communion was the last thing we did together before leaving for the hospital, and we both found it extremely moving, although by this stage I hardly knew whether I was on my head or my heels. Chris especially seemed quite emotional, knowing he was leaving home for a long period, and even possibly for the last time.

Then followed one of those situations which could only be described as coincidental, had we not believed in God's intimate timing for every detail of our lives. I had left the older children with friends, and now had to take Jonathan to a friend who lived a short car drive away. This gave Chris a few moments to himself before leaving. My car, which hadn't been going too well previously, started to choke and splutter going up a hill. I changed to second gear, then first, but finally it stopped. The tears, which were not far away, began to flow, as I wondered how I could ever get Chris to hospital. I prayed for help and then wondered if anyone I knew lived near enough to reach on foot. I thought of the Hewitts just around the corner from where I had stopped, but guessed they'd both be at work. I ran round to their house. And then I just praised God – there was a car in the driveway! Arriving at the door, I met Austin just lifting his keys to go out. When he heard my predicament, he said he had nothing to do that afternoon that couldn't wait. This was unbelievable, especially as he hadn't even planned to be at home for lunch that day – work had finished early and he had just thought he would go home. How perfect was God's timing that the car should have stopped at that exact place at that exact time! When we arrived back at the house, we found that God had even provided company for Chris while I was out. And the journey to hospital was quite pleasant, as Austin in his usual good-humoured way was able to completely lift Chris's somewhat drooping spirits; whereas if I had driven him to hospital myself, we might both have ended up in tears. So it wasn't just the right place at the right time, but the right person too.

This all took place about 12 days in advance of the transplant. First of all, Chris had to have an operation for the insertion of a 'Hickman's line', a tube inserted through his shoulder right into his heart, through which Terence's bone marrow and any drugs or transfusions would pass. The procedure took place the day after he was admitted to hospital, but there were some difficulties and it had to be repeated the next day using the other shoulder. Despite these complications, Chris continued to seem relaxed and confident about everything.

One night, while praying for Chris at home, I had a picture in my mind of him walking along what seemed like the rim of a volcano, with a steep fall on either side; but as I looked, I saw that there were angels on either side, ready to catch him if he should slip. I told him about this as I visited him one evening, and he didn't seem in the least surprised. I certainly had never been in the habit of receiving visions or pictures before, but he just seemed to accept this as something normal for us both at that time.

Over the next few days, Chris was given massive doses of drugs and radiation to reduce the number of white cells in his blood, as they would have to be completely eliminated before he could receive the new bone marrow. During this time I was able to visit him in his side-ward, wearing a face mask to prevent cross-infection, and the staff were most considerate in allowing us longer times together. They knew we would soon be separated, as he eventually would have to go into complete isolation. The children and several of our friends saw him also for periods, and even Jonathan was smuggled in to give a wave from the door. Our solicitor came and finalised the Will with Chris, as in his usual fashion he had left it all to the last minute. Even that did not seem to distress him – it was just something that had to be done. I had realised during the past weeks that he should be doing something about it, but could not bring myself to suggest it.

We also had to discuss with the dietician at this stage, in great detail, what sort of food Chris would be allowed to eat after the transplant: mainly tinned foods, which were sterile.

As the white cells were now being drastically reduced, Chris's resistance to infection was becoming lower, and I knew he would soon have to go into complete isolation. On the last day before that happened, I was told I could be with him for several hours in the afternoon. It was something of a dilemma for me, for although I appreciated the opportunity of having this longer time with him, I really did not look on it as possibly the last time I might ever be close to him or touch him, and I was very conscious of the children needing me too, especially Jonathan, who was still being breast fed. It was, in the end, a fairly tense time for us, as we tried to be relaxed and to make the most of the time we had; yet the longer we were together, the more the implications began to sink in.

The next time we saw Chris, he was in a side ward with a glass partition separating him from the main ward. He had a telephone intercom, through which he communicated with the outside world, which now included me. Only doctors and nurses in sterile gowns were allowed in. Games and books had to be sterilised, and we tried to think of things he could do to pass the time, as he would be confined to that room for several weeks. Sterilising took up to a week, and he realised with some impatience that he would have to wait that time for his daily newspaper! One of the advantages, however, was that Chris now had a private line to his room, with a telephone number which we could use to speak directly to him from home. This was a great help, especially for the children.

There seemed to be nothing at this point which could discourage Chris. He had a cheery smile for everyone who came to see him, and although he was apprehensive and quite realistic about the very daunting procedures he was about to undergo, he faced them with amazing calmness and fortitude. Surely this must be 'the peace which passes all understanding'.

On 31st October, Chris was taken by ambulance to another hospital for his total radiation therapy. This involved being placed in a very cramped position for several hours in a cylinder-shaped container. Knowing how difficult this would be, we borrowed some music tapes from friends, and he found this helped pass the time, though he told me later that he had spent a lot of this time just thinking about us, his family. It was a Sunday, and our church held a 24-hour prayer vigil for him from the Saturday. I am certain this was the reason for his spirits remaining high and the discomfort being kept to a minimum during this unpleasant procedure.

After returning to the isolation ward, Chris was cheerful, but relieved that it was over. The next day, November 1st, he received the transplant as planned, which was not a difficult procedure at all. His brother Terence was in another side-ward, and had previously had the bone marrow removed in theatre from his hip bones – a much more difficult and daunting procedure, performed under anaesthetic using a large bore needle and syringe. This left him feeling very bruised, as if he had been in a very rough rugby match. The transplant was given to Chris in much the same way as a blood transfusion, using the Hickman's line previously inserted, and he continued to be nursed in isolation to prevent infection.

We were warned about problems that might arise later from incompatibility or infection, but the immediate problems were more to do with the side-effects of the radiation: the linings of his mouth, throat and bowel would break down and his hair would later fall out. These problems seemed to be much less than anticipated, and I am sure that this too was due to prayer.

So it was a great shock to everyone, including the doctors, when five days after the radiation and transplant, Chris had some pain and difficulty in breathing, and within minutes of the emergency happening, he was gone.

It was unexpected in that, whereas we knew there could be serious complications, we expected them to occur some time later. When I arrived at the hospital at 7pm as usual that evening, I was shown with a friend into a doctors' room. Yet I didn't seem to think this strange, or wonder why the other visitors were all being kept waiting outside. I chatted for a while to the friend who had also come to see Chris, and although he already suspected that something was wrong, he gave me no clue. So it wasn't until the haematologist, Dr Frank

86

Jones, came in, looking very serious, that I realised that something bad had happened. He himself was so upset he could hardly tell me.

Looking back, I can only see God's hand even in all of this: the older children, Jenny and Niall, seeing him on separate occasions during the week before he died; his mother seeing him just the day before, which coincided with a check-up at the hospital for the hip replacement operation from which she was just recovering; and Jonathan giving him a wave just before he went into isolation. There was also the fact that Chris suffered very little discomfort as he died, whereas had he lived to go through all the side-effects and complications of the actual transplant, he would probably have suffered much more. His chances of surviving were really quite slim (although without the transplant they were even less), so it was good that he had been saved from all those discomforts. We never saw him in pain or losing his hair, which could have been difficult, though we tried to make light of it at the time. God in his great goodness took him when he knew best, and through our prayers was able to use the situation for the best for everyone concerned.

Terence wrote a poem for Chris during the time he was in hospital, expressing his feelings about giving his bone marrow to Chris, a procedure often referred to by the medical profession as a 'bone marrow harvest'.

HARVEST'S HOME by Terence Brown
In memory of Christopher Brown (1946-1982)

Northern light again asserts
Its shocking clarity. I had forgotten!
Snow waits in the wings, a month or two
Will see, for sure, the drifting cells

Slip   from   a   darkened   sky.
And   the   infinite,   crystalline   modes
Of cold perfection petrify your life

With exact termination.

It's   enough   to   make   you   abandon   thought
And   imagine   instead   all   the   composure   of   harvest,
Oozing   like   sap   in   the   tall-boned   trees
Of   spring,   where   we   began,   oh   mothering   earth.
How can harvest come from such fragilities – seeds, buds,
smiles,   fear?
How   can   planting   in   the   earth's   flesh
Bear fruit in grain-fields and apple-ripe counties?

How   do   things   find   their   ways   home?
Travellers   in   snowstorms?
Cells in a bloodstream?

Love in a sweat of fright? Grain to the granary?

O Death, Where is Thy Sting?

My immediate reaction to what had happened was that I just couldn't believe it or take it in at all. Then the tears came and, numb though I was, I was glad I could cry. Our friend Bob went off to find Betty, who had brought me to the hospital that evening. She was already back from parking the car, and the doctors had just told her the news. The nurses brought in tea and Betty wept with me. Soon she went to phone John Ross, and in very little time he was there. He too was obviously very upset, as he had known Chris and myself since soon after we were married. I felt surrounded with love and sympathy from the very moment I heard Chris had died. The doctor was trying to explain what had happened, but I couldn't really take it in. I just kept praying for help, and John and Bob both prayed for me too. Later we were taken in to see Chris's body. It seemed to me only the outer casing of the real, living person I had known and loved. But he did look very peaceful. The doctors kept wanting to explain things to me, but it just didn't seem to matter to me how it had happened. All that mattered was that Chris was gone. I started to wonder how I could ever tell his mother and brother. John Ross took me in his car straight to Chris's mother's house, and went to the door to say that there was bad news. Then I came in and told her, which was one of the hardest things I have ever had to do. She was remarkably calm, and more concerned about me. Betty, who had followed, and knew her well, stayed with her for a while, and John took me home. His wife, Betty Ross, was already at the house, and so was Ian Taylor, our elder.

The children were dancing round in high spirits when I came in. I just said, 'I have to tell you something,' and burst into tears. 'Daddy's gone to be with Jesus.'

Jenny burst out, 'What! What?' then, 'He's not dead, I don't believe it!' (exactly my reaction), then, 'Why?'

I held them both, and they were quite hysterical, though Niall said nothing. Ian talked to them for a while, answering their questions. My mother, father and brother arrived soon, all visibly shaken.

John was starting to think of the practicalities, and asked me if I wanted to think of a Bible verse to put in the morning paper. I couldn't think of anything at that moment, so he left it for a while. Then I thought I should perhaps look through my Bible, and my eye fell on a verse which I had underlined in the Living Bible paraphrase: 'You have given him the unquenchable joy of your presence' (Psalm 21 v.8). I knew then that that was exactly what I wanted to use.

My brother Arthur decided to stay overnight with me, and to help with the funeral arrangements. Ian, John and Betty had left, and Roy Miller arrived. Jenny and Niall wanted to sleep with me, and we got Niall up to bed, but Jenny would not go until I was going. She brought down her Bible and Bible-reading notes (Young People's Every Day with Jesus) and sat between Roy and me. The subject was how the Psalms are full of emotions, and that God wants us to express our emotions to Him, whatever they may be. It was very appropriate, and should have helped us all very much. Eventually we got to bed, but didn't get much sleep, with two and sometimes three children in the bed.

The next day I had a steady stream of visitors. Niall was to go to the zoo with his Beaver pack, and we let him go, as he seemed to want life to continue in its usual routine. Jenny wanted to be with me, and Janet Taylor took Jonathan for long periods. My cousin Lynn came in the evening and was a great comfort to me, and Arthur was able to go home.

The following day was Sunday, and I felt I would like to go to church, especially as it was Communion, though I realised it might make it difficult for other people if I were there. However, I was glad I did go, and I hope nobody minded, as it was a wonderful service. Ian Taylor led the prayers, and I felt they were all meant for us. The children, their granny and I cried through them, and they were so moving that I'm sure many others did too. The choir sang the Aaronic blessing, and through it expressed the love which was surrounding and enfolding us that morning:

> *'The Lord bless thee and keep thee.*
> *The Lord make his face to shine upon thee,*
> *And be gracious unto thee.*
> *The Lord lift up the light of his countenance upon thee,*
> *And give thee peace.'*

I am still strongly moved every time I hear or sing it.

We all had lunch with the Millars, and the children then went to friends' houses, while I went home to see more visitors. Everything seemed very strange to me at this stage, as if it were all happening to someone else. I found about half an hour to pray before going to the Ross's for tea. During those few days, I found I seldom had a moment to myself for anything.

The funeral was to be on Tuesday, and on the Monday morning, Betty Ross came round and helped tidy up the house for it. There were still a lot of callers, and after lunch Betty suggested I go to bed for an hour, something I never normally do during the day. What kindness and caring I received from so many people at that time. Chris's brother Terence and his family arrived later that day, to stay for the funeral.

What a strange yet wonderful day was the day of the funeral. From the very start the Lord's presence was all about me. Various elders' wives came and went, organising cups, soup and cakes (which were constantly arriving) and seeing that the house was ready. A neighbour offered to look after the children, plus my nephew and niece Michael and Carolyn, though Jenny, Niall and Michael were to come to the service with us. It was a cool, bright, crisp November day. I wore my new culotte suit and, at someone's suggestion, took a jacket for the cemetery. I wanted to look well in Chris's honour – he'd have appreciated that more than all the flowers, I thought. Terence and his mother arrived then – he had slept at her house. She was calm, but fussing over small details. Terence was able to reassure her in a gentle way. The car then took us all the short distance to the church.

Strong emotions rose in me as I entered our beloved church. But I checked the tears just then, as I wanted so much to behave with dignity for the children's sake, so that they would know they had someone strong to lean upon, and also for my own sake, so that I could get the most benefit from the service without being overcome with emotion. Our organist Ronnie Hiscocks was playing 'He shall feed his flock' so sensitively. I was aware that I was surrounded by probably most of the people who had ever meant anything to me in my whole life, for many people had come some distance to be there. The love and sympathy in that church was almost tangible. When our minister John Ross rose to speak, his voice was filled with emotion. A small group of our friends sang the words from Isaiah 43, 'Fear not, for I have redeemed you', which included the lines:

> *'When you walk through the waters, I will be with you, and through rivers – they will not overwhelm you. When you walk through the fire, you will not be burned, the flames shall not consume you.'*

This was a steadying influence on us all. The sermon was preached by Roy Millar, an elder, and the climax of his message came when he said, 'Chris is not dead! He is more alive than we are!' And when he spoke directly to the children, Terence and Mrs Brown, we felt again that surge of love from those around us. Ian Taylor's prayer which followed was like poetry, and through it I felt lifted to heaven itself. The sorrow was so deep, and yet the joy unimaginable – it felt like a foretaste to me of what heaven might be like. (I have shown this prayer, along with Ian's communion address, at the end of the chapter, as they are words I will want to remember always).

Both of the hymns chosen were full of meaning for me: the first, 'Be still, my soul', because it had spoken to me at choir practice just after I learned that Chris had leukaemia, although I had found it hard to look at since then. But I knew it had to be the one – every word expressed how I felt now. Only weeks later did it occur to me that the tune 'Finlandia' was one of Chris's favourite pieces of music. The final hymn, 'Thine be the glory', finished the service on a note of triumph. It was the hymn that Chris's mother wished to be included, and also one of my own favourites. How could anyone singing it not be drawn to the Prince of Life, who makes us more than conquerors, as He Himself has conquered death! Only He makes sense of living and dying.

Coming back down the aisle, there were so many people reaching out to us in love. I couldn't speak to many just then, and was glad to get into the car and move off; too much in a world of my own at that moment to communicate with people. At the Maypole in the town centre, the police stood to attention and saluted. The flag was at half-mast. Passing the house again was an emotional moment. As I was leaving the church, I had been given a small brown envelope, and I used this time to open it and read the little verse inside. They were comforting words, which helped me concentrate my mind on God again. I found out later that it was sent by Mr Alex Finlay, a senior member of our church. As his contribution, this was as valuable to me as any, yet so humbly given. The passage came from St Francis de Sales:

A thought for today:

'Do not look forward to the changes and chances of this life in fear; rather look to them with full hope that as they arise, God whose you are will deliver you out of them. He has kept you hitherto, do you but hold fast to His dear hand, and He will lead you safely through all things, and when you cannot stand, He will bear you in his arms. What need you fear, my child, remembering that you are God's and that He has said, "All things work together for good to those that love Him."

'Do not look forward to what may happen tomorrow. The same Everlasting Father who cares for you today will take care of you tomorrow and every day. Either He will shield you from suffering; or He will give you unfailing strength to bear it. Be at peace then, put aside all anxious thoughts and imaginings, and say continually "The Lord is my strength and my shield; my heart has trusted in Him and I am helped." He is not only with me but in me, and I in Him. What can a child fear, surrounded by such a Father's arm?'

The trees along the road were all red and gold against a pale blue sky. It was cold, but the car was warm and comfortable. Its slow progress lulled me into a peaceful state, and I felt I never wanted to leave its womb-like interior. As we reached the cemetery, I came back to reality, and found that now I wanted to go and speak to each person who had come, most of whom were very dear friends. It occurred to me that perhaps other widows might wait for others to approach them, but I was not aware of the rules, and did as my heart dictated, and I was blessed by each contact.

Back at the house, a fire was blazing to welcome the 40-50 guests, and the ladies of the church served soup and sandwiches, sausages, tea and cakes. It was good to meet and talk with Chris's cousins from England, and also many of our own dearest friends whom I had not seen for some time.

APPENDICES TO CHAPTER 3

Appendix A

IAN TAYLOR'S PRAYER AT COMMUNION

Philippians 4 verse 13
I can do everything through him who gives me strength.
Lord, I can only bear the loss of Chris through the strength You give me. I know I can only bring Jenny and Niall and Jonathan up in your nurture through the strength you are giving me. You know there will be times when I will feel terribly alone, times when I will cry and weep openly before you who gives me strength. O Lord, my Lord, my comforter, Chris's Redeemer, my soul is weary with sorrow, strengthen me according to your word. *Psalm 1J9 v. 28.*

Isaiah 41 verse 10
(So) do not fear, for l am with you, do not be dismayed, for I am your God. I will strengthen you and help you; I will uphold you with my righteous hand. Do not be afraid.
Strengthen Jenny and Niall and Jonathan too, Father.

Psalm 116 verse 15

Precious in the sight of the Lord is the death of his saints. O Lord I am your servant; I am your servant, the son of your maidservant; you have freed me from my chains.

Lord, we thank you that Chris is in your sight and that you are in Chris's. He is your servant still, you have freed him from his chains, the chains of an ill body, you have freed him from his earthly to his heavenly home. We pray for Mrs Brown and Mr and Mrs Anderson and their families, for your comfort for them and their faith and hope in you.

2 Timothy 4 verses 8 and 6

Now there is in store for me the crown of righteousness, which the Lord, the righteous judge, will award to me on that day – and not only to me, but also to all who have longed for his appearing.

For I am already being poured out like a drink offering, and the time has come for my departure. I have fought the good fight, I have finished the race, I have kept the faith.

Lord, restore the faith which crumbles with the news of death. You have defeated death – give us your hope, give us your faith.

Proverbs 3 verse 5

Trust in the Lord with all your heart, and lean not on your own understanding.

Lord, times like this are beyond our understanding. Help us to run to you and to trust in you with all our heart. Help those who feel that you are a spiteful God who takes young people away, for we know that you are a God of compassion, that you feel our grief.

John 16 verses 20 and 22

I tell you the truth, you will weep and mourn while the world rejoices. You will grieve, but your grief will turn to joy. Now is your time of grief but I will see you again and you will rejoice, and no one will take away your joy

Father, thank you for giving us tears to share with one another, thank you for giving us the ability to grieve that stops our hearts from breaking, thank you that with grief there is also joy, the deep joy of knowing Chris is safe with you. You are wiping away our tears, Father, You are taking away sorrows and suffering, You are taking us to be with You in eternal glory.

Romans 14 verse 8
Whether we live or die, we belong to the Lord.

2 Corinthians 5 verses 1, 7 and 8
Now we know that if this earthly tent we live in is destroyed, we have a building from God, an eternal house in heaven, not built by human hands. We live by faith, not by sight. We are confident, I say, and would prefer to be away from the body and at home with the Lord.
For we are strangers, Father, sojourners on this earth. Give us the knowledge of you that our deepest desire might be for all of us to be with You. Instead of a fear of death, may we greet it with the joy of knowing we are entering your presence.

1 Thessalonians 5 verse 10
He died for us so that, whether we are awake or asleep, we may live together with Him. Therefore, encourage one another and build each other up, just in fact as you are doing.

Father, you are the God of the living, and the Living God. You are not the great I WAS but the great I AM, neither is Chris a person who was, but a person who is. He has laid off the physical body and You have clothed him with eternal righteousness. Help us while we remain in these frail vessels we call our bodies, to encourage and build one another up.

I am the resurrection and the life. No one can come to the father except by me.

Life - that's where Chris has gone from here.

To life
To eternal life
To eternal joy
To eternal peace
To the father.

Let not your hearts be sorrowful, but set your hearts on following to where Chris has gone. You know the way to the place where I am going.

In the name and through the grace and mercy of Christ Jesus, our hope. Amen.

Appendix B

IAN TAYLOR'S PRAYER AT CHRIS'S FUNERAL SERVICE

I am not skilled to understand what God hath willed, what God hath planned. I only know, at His right hand Stands One who is my Saviour.

Peace I leave with you, my peace I give you. I do not give to you as the world gives. Do not let your hearts be troubled and do not be afraid.

Come let us to the Lord our God with contrite hearts return. Our God is gracious, nor will He leave the desolate to mourn.

Let us pray.

Footsteps in the sands of life, his and mine, dwelling in perfect harmony, perfect love. Now they say that he is gone. Some don't know where. I do, Lord.

Tears well up, fond remembrances flood through my memory. What did you say to him, Lord?

'Come, you faithful servant of the Lord, and inherit the kingdom prepared for you before the earth was born. I spoke, you heard, you responded. In your hour of need you drew near to me and I to you, you received my presence and my peace into your heart. That presence, that peace took you through that fleeting moment called death, when you cast off the restraints of earth and received your full freedom as my son. Welcome home, son.'

Some say he passed from life to death, Father, some are full of pity for me but no hope. They cannot understand that I can have your joy in my sorrow, your peace in my tribulation. Passed from life to death, Father? Ah no! Passed from death to life! Free of sin and free from disease and free of death, free in Him!

And who is that I see greeting him, Father, dressed in a robe reaching down to his feet and with a golden sash around his chest? With head and hair white like wool, as white as snow and his eyes like blazing fire? With feet like bronze glowing in a furnace, with a voice like the sound of rushing waters. His face like the sun shining

99

in all its brilliance, one like a son of man, saying 'Do not be afraid. I am the First and the Last. I am the Living One. I was dead, and behold I am alive for ever and ever! And I hold the keys of death and Hades.'

Separated but together, Father, united in our faith, our hope, our love of you. These three, faith, hope and love, are eternal; they can never be destroyed. Though the earth were to shatter and the heavens cave in, nothing can separate us from your love, Father, nothing.

This is the victory, Father, and whenever this heaven and this earth have passed away we will be there in your presence. Father, we will be there.

I am my beloved's and he is mine and his banner over me is Love.

Footsteps, footsteps in the sands of eternity, his and mine, dwelling in perfect harmony, perfect love with our Lord, perfect...

Our last photo taken together as a family. Goodbye, my love

Business card for Chris's new business 'Strangford Insulation Products' based in Newtownards

On our last holiday together as a family, in Lanzarote

Chris in the woods

4

LIFE AFTER DEATH

Learning to Adjust

What were the influences that most helped me to adjust to my changed circumstances, especially during the first few months after Chris's death? When I sit down to count them they are many, but by far the most important and valuable to me has been TO KNOW GOD and to live in close communion with Him. When my husband, the one who was, next to God, most important to me, was taken away from me, it made me start to realise that the only thing that can never be taken away from us is God Himself, and He is always accessible, even though we may not always want access. So we should never build our security on any other person, not even our husband or wife, nor on anything material, our home or our possessions, our job, not even our church, but only on Christ. 'In him (alone) we live and move, and have our being.' This should be our base, and everything else is secondary. And so I made a definite decision to throw myself entirely upon God, to put Him to the test, to prove that He was as good as His word. It was an easy decision really – He was all that I had left to turn to, the children being a responsibility He had given me. It may all sound a bit hyper-spiritual, but it was in fact a reality to me, that whenever I turned to God in his Word or in prayer, I began to understand His will and

104

purposes more and more. The more I threw myself upon God, sometimes in wordless prayer, I was first of all uplifted and given a wonderful peace and confidence, and then I was given strength to go ahead and cope with whatever presented itself next. Also, believing that only faith in God mattered kept me from worrying about the material side of things – the liquidation of the business, or how long it would take for the insurance money to start coming in. And God honoured that trust. I have never been in need materially since Chris's death.

I have already mentioned the second most important thing to me at this time: PRAYER. There were times when I felt unable to pray at all, and this was when I was so totally dependent on the prayers of others, which I know were constant, even months afterwards. These prayers, I am sure, carried me through the worst patches, and were the key to my ability to cope against all odds. In my own prayers I found I enjoyed a much closer communion with God than ever before, talking to Him about everything before I would go to sleep, just as I would have done with Chris. There came to be a real sense of His presence, especially in the bedroom where I usually prayed, or in front of the fire late at night after friends had left. In this the Lord was like a husband to me, as in the line of a hymn, 'Jesus, my husband, shepherd, friend...' Personal worship has become a very important part of prayer to me, as I consider how wonderfully God has helped me through these months.

Whereas talking to God in prayer helped replace the 'sounding-board' aspect of the marriage relationship, BOOKS became a kind of companionship to me. Though not such an effective two-way relationship as either prayer or marriage, in a way I gave something of myself in the choosing of what to read and what to reject, and I certainly received much in return. In fact this was one way in which God was able to speak to me, through both the Bible and other books. One I found particularly helpful was Where Eagles Soar by Jamie Buckingham. I had read this when Chris was ill, but its theme stayed with me and helped me soar on the wings of prayer, by the breath of the Holy Spirit, above the turbulence of my life beneath. Several books by other widows were also helpful: To Live Again by Catherine Marshall; Be Still my Soul by Elizabeth Urch; The Ones who are Left, an article by Elizabeth Elliott; A Severe Mercy by Sheldon Vanauken (a widower); and also, Don't Waste your Sorrows by Paul Bilheimer, about why Christians are not exempt from suffering. Living Light, a book of daily Scripture readings based on the Living Bible, was given to me by a friend at this time and was invaluable, as were the Every Day With Jesus Bible-reading notes, which Chris and I had both been reading for a few months, and which during November and December 1982 were on the subject of 'Finding Grace in the Dungeon'. One week they were on loneliness, and another week on grief. Through these notes I was led to parts of the Bible where I could find help, and was often amazed at the timing of appropriate passages. In the Bible I found the Psalms a great comfort, also 1 Peter and parts of Isaiah chapters 40, 43, 45, 54 and 61, and many other passages.

Equally valuable to me was the depth of LOVE AND FRIENDSHIP I received from those I knew, especially my Christian friends. To me, they were a part of the Body of Christ, and through them He was able to minister to me. This ranged from spiritual help from many of our church elders, who counselled me through my worst times, to practical help: caring for the children for periods; repairs and maintenance to my house; hospitality and advice. But there were also those who 'just' prayed, or stopped to talk, or brought a friend who was also a widow, or those who did not know what to say but communicated their love by a squeeze of the hand or even just a look. Mr Finlay's little verse, for example, was a real help to me on the way to the cemetery.

The CHILDREN were and always would be a wonderful help, as I looked to the way ahead. In the immediate sense, they kept me busy, and my life tended to revolve around them, as indeed it had to a certain extent already. For their continuing security, which I saw as very important, life had to go on as much as possible the same as before. I felt that although God might have another eventual purpose for my life, I didn't have to look too far for one right then, for the children provided a ready-made purpose: to look after their daily needs and help them consider the future as they grew up.

It has also been a wonderful ASSURANCE to know that I will see Chris again in heaven, that he is not gone for good; and I know that is also a help to the children. Sometimes I have wondered if he knows how I am coping. I felt he would want me to get on with living, even enjoy life again, and not get too depressed because he wasn't there. He was always one for implementing change, and I hope I implemented this change in my life as he would have liked me to.

MUSIC came to mean more to me in those months, as indeed it did to Chris just before he died. I found that after the children went to bed there was often a quiet opportunity to listen. It has the power to soothe the emotions or stir the memories or, as with sacred music, to help me concentrate my mind in the right direction. 'The Swan' by Saint-Saëns was a piece I loved to listen to on my own.

TEARS – some people who see me outside may think that I am not emotional, but with me tears are not something just below the surface all the time, ready to start when someone speaks to me. They usually just come when I am alone and can really let go. At these times, I would end up just reaching out for help in an agonised sort of prayer, help which I found always came. I have read that in

107

weeping a substance is released in the tears which has a beneficial effect, and I know I always feel more relaxed and content after allowing myself a 'good cry'. There is always a feeling too of being nearer to God. However, in my experience the dividing line is thin between tears of normal grief and tears of self-pity, and I feel it is important not to indulge in the latter, as self-pity only leaves bitterness and negative feelings. This is one reason why prayer is so important at these times.

TALKING about my feelings, or writing them down in a journal or in letters to friends, has been therapeutic for me. I have been fortunate in having many 'willing ears' to listen to me pour out my feelings – though if I do this too much, I get tired of listening to the same old record, and feel the listeners may do so too. Occasionally, some people may have probed sensitive areas, and I have learnt by experience to change the subject when I know this could happen. Otherwise, especially at the beginning, I would start to dwell on issues raised which I wasn't quite ready to think about. I record events and feelings, as I know I have a dreadful memory for details, and it may prove useful to refer to in future in order to be of help to people in similar circumstances.

Some recently bereaved people find GOING TO CHURCH difficult. Perhaps they are afraid they will show their emotions, but what better place could there be to remove all barriers and allow God to speak and console in a deep and meaningful way? As I have described above, my first Sunday service after Chris died took place before his funeral, and was especially moving for me as it was a Communion service. I was aware that I was not the only one who wept that morning. The prayer of intercession, led by Ian Taylor, was addressed to us as a family, and when the choir then sang the Aaronic Blessing (completely unexpectedly), it was an inexpressibly moving moment. Since then, other services have also been moving, and I have often felt the words of hymns, prayers or sermon seemed to be addressed specifically to me. I believe this is one way in which God does speak in order to make His way clearer to us. I joined the choir again in the new year, two months after Chris had died, and also the Come and Worship singing group (despite some criticism!), as I found praising God for His greatness was a positive help to me.

I have many 'props' in evidence around the house which help to keep my spirits up. I have various Bible posters, one saying 'The wonder of His love compels me to reach out with Jesus'; and there are small stickers in odd places saying things like 'Keep hoping', 'Hallelujah anyway!', 'Sing life, sing love!' etc. Words of hymns that have been especially meaningful to me are pinned on the kitchen notice-board, for example 'Be still, my soul'; and an old hymn by Isaac Watts, 'Sweet is the work, my God and King'; and the words of the metrical paraphrase of Psalm 22, verses 3-5. The passage by St Francis de Sales starting, 'Do not look forward to the changes and chances of this life in fear,' which Mr Finlay had sent me on the day of the funeral, was very helpful to me. I read these words many, many times, and they seemed to sum up my trust in God over this time.

Six months after the event, I felt like I'd been on my own for much longer, so much had happened in that time. Although I had always been responsible for the running of the household, including bills and bank statements, there were certain areas that I knew very little about, for example tax, insurance and investment of money, as well as house maintenance. However, I was able to get expert help on most of these, or learned to do it myself. I had a headstone engraved; I served on the school management committee; friends, children and church groups kept me grounded in the world around. Grief, when it came, was just as painful, but it came less often. Sometimes it related to missing Chris himself; but I found I was getting more used to that, and learning to ask myself in difficult situations, 'What would Chris do or think?' So he was still with me in spirit. More often I got upset about just being alone, and feeling I needed that one-to-one relationship. In this I have been very fortunate in having some good friends, with whom I can completely be myself – something I never thought could happen again.

In the succeeding months and even years, I found I had various problems that related directly to my widowhood, and I can say confidently that in all of these God has been able to gently lead me through them until a solution is found. Often all it needs is time, and so I wait, knowing that He is with me in the waiting. There were various occurrences that were so much associated with Chris that when they happened I couldn't bear them. Certain television programmes he enjoyed, such as Yes, Minister and rugby internationals, I found quite impossible to watch for over a year. Even news bulletins and current affairs programmes were difficult, but I made myself get used to them, as I did not want to cut myself off entirely from the world outside. A radio programme on consumer affairs, which had attacked Chris's business while he was ill, was anathema to me. And I couldn't eat prawns, although I loved them, as I had a theory that Chris's fondness for them might have contributed to his illness. Superstitious, you may think? These things are very real to the bereaved person, even a Christian.

I found the children's grief difficult. I knew they had to cry too, yet it hurt me so much to see them suffer that I avoided encouraging them to talk about Chris at first. Various books showed me this was wrong, and we learned to voice our thoughts and weep together. I found it easier to talk to Jonathan, who was just a toddler, about his daddy going to heaven, as I could do that without the emotional overtones of talking to the older two.

It is well-known that bereaved people often dream of their loved ones who have died, and I have been no exception to this. However, I find that my dreams fall into two categories. The first type occurred right from the week that Chris died, and in them it is as if he had never left, that life was just as it had been. I would waken, feeling momentarily that he was still with me, only to experience immediately the sudden devastating realisation that he was gone for good. These dreams were quite upsetting at first, but later I grew to savour their memory, just for the pleasure of feeling that he had been with me, if only in mind. The second type of dream did not occur until exactly a year after Chris died, and was totally different. These dreams occurred many times, and in them Chris seemed to come to me from somewhere else in order to teach me something specific. I can only describe each in detail, in order to try and convey what I mean.

1. 30 October 1983: I dreamed I glanced through the garden door and saw Chris standing there in the gateway, his head and shoulders covered with a veil. This did not seem at all strange, and his clothing was perfectly ordinary. As he approached, the veil vanished, and I was amazed at his appearance. His hair was golden, and his face and bearing were full of health and beauty. I wanted to speak, but no sounds came. It seemed as if he had been lost, gone away for the year, perhaps suffered from amnesia, and had somehow found his way back to us, his family. What joy, I thought, he would see how the children had grown and developed! We reached out for each other, and as we embraced, he was gone, and I was awake.... When I looked in the mirror, I was ugly

with weeping. But it came to me that I was being given a glimpse of how he was now, that he had a new body, the disease was gone, and he had no more pain. As I contemplated this, I realised that God was showing me that he was now with God, and my small worry that he had never been baptised disappeared and was of no consequence. Chris's presence was with me very much all that day, especially in church (as it was a Sunday, which I felt was no coincidence). It was as if he was saying to me, 'Yes, I am with Christ, I have a new body which is perfectly whole. I am fully healed, and I wanted to show you something of the glory which is in heaven, and to reassure you that I am there.'

2. The second dream occurred about three months later, and was not quite so dramatic. In it I was taken to a Christian musical or concert in Belfast by someone who seemed to be Chris, although I did not recognise him at first. After the concert was over, we could not find my car in the car park where we had left it. It seemed to have been stolen, and I was getting quite upset and talking about getting the police. Then I noticed that Chris was quite unperturbed, and would have been content to walk home, and leave the problem unsolved. There was an 'other-worldliness' about him, but I knew I was to learn from him not to allow myself to become in any way attached to or dependent on any material possessions. I have since determined to simplify my lifestyle, though Satan immediately attacked me with a temptation to buy an expensive 'Sunday' suit, which I knew I could not keep, and returned to Marks and Spencer the following day!

3. September 1988: This was a vivid dream in which I was pregnant and in hospital about to have a baby. Chris was

coming to see me, but I sensed something was wrong between us. He came in looking very dapper the day before the birth. He said he would come again next day after the baby was born. He kissed me on the cheek. I felt his skin was smooth. He showed no emotion about seeing me after so long a time. I had a sudden doubt, and asked him, 'Are you seeing someone else?' He answered 'Yes'. I woke up immediately, feeling devastated and deeply hurt, and wept most of the morning.

4. May 1989: I dreamed I heard Chris was in prison on a long sentence, but Jenny or Mum heard he was getting out on remission. She managed to get to speak to him on the phone, and even got Jonathan to speak to him, unknown to me. He told me he remembered his Daddy's voice. Then I was to go and see him in a flat somewhere. It was dimly lit. He was very subdued and very pale – we cried a lot and hugged each other. It must have been Jenny who found him, because then we heard Mum wanted to see him, but I sensed Chris didn't want to see her. However, she came, and he hid in the shower, but she got in and saw him briefly, then left. Someone came bringing clothes, but he didn't want them. Besides, they were too small, more like children's clothes. We kept two items anyway to get rid of this very insistent sales lady. It seemed as if it were all to be kept secret that he was out – probably he didn't want people to see him in such a state. Then it seemed my mum had caused a bad car accident in the street outside, and was trying to get back in. Two cars were involved, and someone was hurt, but she was trying to hide, and I had to get the police and help put traffic cones round the cars, all the while knowing Chris was in the

flat and wanting to keep Mum away from him. She was saying things like she was going to kill him on the spot where he had killed someone else (probably why he had been in prison). Other details were fuzzy, but I woke up feeling very protective toward him. His helplessness was very evident; I was the strong one.

5.In dreams that kept recurring before October 1995, Chris had suffered a mental illness, and needed help to readjust back.

6.During the same period: It was as if he had lost his memory, and was living somewhere else, but overjoyed to be re-united.

7.Again before 1995: He was wandering around the world, looking for us.

8.Throughout the 1990s there were further recurring dreams, vague and poorly remembered. I was speaking to him on the phone; arranging to meet somewhere; awaking with a desire to speak with him again… but this time I was not upset about it.

9.There were also dreams throughout this period of just being with him – no heavy overtones of mental or memory problems or other women…

10.Spring 1999: There was vague talk that Chris was coming back. No one knew when, or where he had been. I was with friends in a room when he arrived at the door, but he had changed so much I hardly knew him. He said he knew this would create difficulties for me and for John (a friend who by that time had become my current partner), and I did not know what I would do, loving them both as I did. I woke unresolved.

11.June 1999: I attended a reading of Enoch Arden at the Mussenden Temple, read by Margaret D'Arcy. I knew I would dream about Chris after it, because of the theme of Enoch returning, after being assumed dead, to find his wife had remarried. Not that night but the next, I dreamed Chris came back, and I was torn between him and John, but the details were vague, and I could not recall them.

Christmas Memories

In November 1987, I wrote in my diary of the memories playing around my mind:

Four (five?) years have passed since that November evening when my life changed and I became a widow. But oh! it seems much longer. Our life together seems to slip through my fingers like a piece of fine silk. I try to clutch the fabric, but it becomes fragmented in my grasp. Some memories remain strong as cotton, others hang on a thread like a piece of cobweb. The conversations with friends; the times of closeness; the way he brushed his teeth; his smile; his certain stance. Strong, enduring memories.

We took Christmas very much for granted. He never shopped till Christmas Eve, by which time I had all mine done. Strangely, the gifts we gave each other are mostly all forgotten. As Christmas catalogues arrive, I see the things I'd love to give him now. Christmas morning was always an early start. We groaned together at the three o'clock shrieks of delight and tearing of papers round the fireplace where last night's embers still glowed. I try so hard to recall every detail of the day, but all that comes to mind is the sense of family togetherness, our own small unit, and the wonder of the incarnation.

This year we are in a new house. It's not a matter of trying to make it seem the same as it used to be. It never could, so there is a sense of relief in being able to start afresh. The enduring qualities would still be there, yet each year their poignancy pulled at my emotions. The carol singing, the careful wrapping of presents, the Christ-child, and oh, the warmth of fellowship as our church family meets for family worship on Christmas morning, helping in immense measure to calm the loneliness that cries out so much more at Christmas. Back home, grandparents, uncles, aunts, gather for the meal, each one sensing the empty chair. Yet to me he is there; I could almost touch him.

Thank you, Lord, for 13 happy Christmases together, three children each displaying some beloved characteristic of his or her own, and countless caring friends and family. Life is still worth the living!

Melmore

Soon after Chris's diagnosis, Jonathan was discovered to have an inguinal hernia, which was operated on in the Ulster Hospital. I had to stay with him as he was still being breast fed. Unfortunately, parents were not given much encouragement to stay with a child back then, so it was quite stressful for me.

That summer we had booked a short holiday at the Carrigart Hotel in Donegal, and as soon as Jonathan was discharged we set off. His carrycot had to be propped up in the back of the estate car to allow any fluid to drain. Unknown to us, that would be our last holiday together as a family. One day we set out in the car to find a nice beach to spend the day. At a fork in the road, Chris wanted to go straight on, probably to a place we had been before, but I pointed out that there was a heavy rain cloud in that direction, while the road to the right was heading towards a beautiful blue sky. For once I won the argument. We knew that there were people from our church in Holywood who had caravans there, and I suspected Chris wanted the holiday to be just us as a family, but he agreed to turn right, and that was how we found the wonderful beaches around the headland at Melmore Head. Each had different aspects and types of sand: some soft sand, others rough or rounded stones. There we found many people we knew, who were also aware of our situation, and they were so kind without seeming to pity us. The sun shone, the children played in the sand and swam in the sea. Chris was offered a boat trip out in the bay, and the whole weekend turned out to be a complete success.

By next summer, Chris was gone, and we were contemplating how we would spend the summer months. I asked the children if they would like to go back to that lovely beach in Donegal where we had gone with Daddy, and they quickly agreed. Soon a good friend took me to look at some touring caravans. I bought a small four-berth caravan and the car acquired a tow hook. Another friend gave me a quick lesson in driving with a caravan attached, including the tricky bit – reversing into a small space! We tried it out on a short trip to Melmore.

Our first full summer holiday at Melmore was full of promise and expectation. We were sad, but I knew I had to keep going somehow, and even start to find some fun and joy in life. Fresh air and a change of scenery is always a good antidote to grief, and with the help of some good friends we set about making the best of what life had thrown at us.

We felt ready to go, but I was worried about my brother-in-law and his family. Terence now had only his mother as family, and she was going downhill with Alzheimer's. He wasn't coping well with the loss of his brother, and the fact he had unsuccessfully contributed his bone marrow hadn't helped. His wife Sue was also finding it hard to cope with the situation, as her own family were far away in America, and she had been admitted to hospital. Their two children, Michael and Carolyn (known as Linski), were still very young and it had been suggested they might have to call social services regarding their care. Without thinking very hard, I offered to have them come stay with me. It was the beginning of summer, and Michael was still at school, but our own primary school in Holywood was happy to take him for the last weeks of the summer term, and Carolyn stayed with us at home. It all happened quite suddenly, but when school finished, we were keen to get away to this wonderful beach, and the caravan we had just purchased. A friend kindly towed the van to Donegal and had it set in place before we arrived, and I followed in my Mini Metro with five children and a fortnight's food supplies. We took a tent too, as the caravan was only a four-berther.

We were given a spot just inside the entrance to the caravan site, which was not as other commercial caravan sites in Northern Ireland: these have electric lighting and communal toilets! Our site was just a farmer's field, rented out to tourists in the summer for extra income. However, I had absolutely no experience of caravanning, and just took things as they came along. We had purchased a Porta Potti, and must have had some sort of toilet tent – I can't remember now. But we were expecting sunshine and maybe the odd shower of rain – it was summer after all! Perhaps we were forgetting it was Northern Ireland. As we started erecting the tent, the rain began. As night fell, Jonathan, Carolyn, Jenny and I settled in the van, with the older boys, Niall and Michael, in the tent. And the rain got worse.

I started to consider I had been crazy to take on these extra children. I must have been on a roll, with no expectation of any sort of calamity. But now I thought, how would I cope with five children, with their individual food issues, in a small space where we had little kitchen equipment? The cousins expected chips with everything, and there was no deep fat fryer. Our friends on the site were sympathetic and helpful when they could be, but in reality it was up to me to feed and care for these five children. It rained for a few more days, and we even considered going back home, until suddenly we woke one morning to find the sun beaming in through the caravan windows. And from then on it was the most wonderful holiday! The Dublin children, being ginger-haired and fair-skinned, had to stay in the caravan out of the strong sun around midday, but other than that, they were on the beach, in the water, and fully enjoying the freedom of life on a remote caravan site in Donegal – no television or trashy shops, just having fun outdoors.

And for the next few summers, as soon as school finished, we set off for Donegal. We would look forward to renewing friendships we had made the previous year. Our little Mini Metro used to groan its way up the steep hill of the Glenshane Pass, speed slackening with the gradient and the weight of the caravan, while the people in the car in front laughed and gesticulated through their rear window. As it was a touring caravan, I towed it back home at the end of each summer and parked it in the driveway until the next year.

One day, Jenny and some of her friends took a walk to the 'Boulder Beach', which was as its name suggests covered in rounded stones and pebbles, hard to walk on and more remote, so not often visited by people on walks. And while there, Jenny found a plastic bottle sealed with black tape. Examining it, and thinking it might have a letter in it, she opened it up. And yes, there was indeed a letter inside! It was from a ship's captain from Newfoundland, and this is what he wrote:

> '45*06'N   50*00'W
>
> *The Person who picks up this plastic bottle, please Contact Tony Bennett in Trepassey phone number 438-2554 this was threw into the water on the S.E. South East side off the Sand Banks of Nfld, Canada by the Captain of the "Zory" T.B.*
>
> | *Fishing* | *Trawler* | *March* | *14th* | *1984.'* |
> |---|---|---|---|---|
> | *And* | *on* | *the* | *back* | *was* | *written:* |
>
> | '*A* | *reward* | *of* | *$20* | *is* | *offered.* |
> |---|---|---|---|---|---|
> | *Phone* | | - | | | *438-2554* |
>
> *Write – Tony Bennett, Trepassey, Southern Shore, Newfoundland, Canada'*

We wrote to him, Jenny hoping in due course to receive her €20. We corresponded with Tony for several years, and received pictures of his family and a new baby named Victoria. Christmas cards were exchanged each year, until a letter told us that Tony had had a heart attack and died. His wife continued to correspond for a while, but she was coping alone now with the new baby, and the letters stopped. Then one day in 2011, a couple came to my door in Holywood, Northern Ireland, and the girl said she was the baby in the story! She is now a friend on Facebook, and we still have the letter!

Norah at a friend's wedding in 1990

At a family wedding: from left - Zoe, Lindsay, Doreen, Arthur, Nik, Sancha, and Liz Anderson, Jonathan, Jenny and Norah Brown

Jenny holding Jonathan and Niall in our home at Tudor Oaks, Holywood

5

WHAT WOULD JESUS DO?

You can never tell the sort of dilemmas life is going to throw

up at you. Here was I, a conscientious Christian wife, happily involved in homemaking and bringing up a family of three kids. Then wham! leukaemia enters, and within eight months my only-ever lover and father of my children was gone. It certainly set me back in my tracks.

My mother's greatest wish for me was that I should never do anything wrong. I had made my own commitment at the age of seven to give my life to God and be guided by what He laid down in the Bible. This I realised was frequently open to interpretation, but what my Brethren upbringing taught me was: no sex before marriage; no sex outside marriage; and sex only within marriage. All these we had observed, though our engagement had been particularly fraught, as we tried and actually succeeded in avoiding intercourse. But I couldn't remember any teaching or guidelines on my Christian position in life as a widow with two schoolchildren and a baby. So I searched my Bible and was shocked by St Paul's condescending and misogynistic attitude to women in general. Looking for guidance, I attended a weekend for Christian widows and gained some interesting insights from English and American speakers.

I missed the companionship, the support of a second parent and, yes, the sexual side. The first could be partially helped by the friendship of people I knew, and to some extent also the second. But the third was a problem. So marriage seemed the only option. However, just keeping things running along took much of my time, and I never seemed to have the opportunity to meet any likely new men. But for 10 years I was privileged to have the friendship of some of the most unlikely companions…

Chris's year group at Sullivan Upper School were an interesting bunch. I had met many of them and even become accepted as part of the group. Chris had a great affection for several. Two of these friends, Bob and Ian, had gone abroad and I hadn't really met them. However, it just so happened that around the time Chris was ill, these two found themselves back home in Holywood. And naturally, being good friends of his, they were alarmed and worried at someone they knew well, of their own age, being suddenly affected by a potentially fatal disease. They were frequent visitors and it was good for him to renew old friendships at a time when he deeply appreciated them.

Bob had been head boy, a clever scholar, but was never involved with the Christian Union, which Chris belonged to. He had questioned Christianity at a deep intellectual level, and had eventually become something of a hippie, and followed a hippie lifestyle in America. But while travelling in Nigeria he met some Christian missionaries and became converted. Back home again, he was a zealous proselytiser for his new-found faith. He now felt he should be on the lookout for a good Christian wife! Unfortunately for him, he did not appeal to me in this way, but he did become a good friend, always ready for an intellectual discussion. On the practical front he was not much help, though he was strong and could always lift or move things for me. He would visit me in the evenings after the children had gone to bed, asking probing questions about my feelings on God, healing, prayer, the church, ecumenism, marriage, women's place in the church. He helped bring to the surface a lot of the unspoken feelings I had about Chris and the events surrounding his illness and death.

Then there was Ian. Ian was a true eccentric.

Perhaps because my parents seemed unduly influenced by what other people thought, I became fascinated by eccentrics. They just seemed more interesting to me. Chris had been eccentric to some extent – he didn't care what people thought of him, but everyone liked him anyway. Ian was so eccentric that people gave up trying to understand him. He would talk about his travels and the people he had met, occasionally lapsing into French and other languages, but somehow managing to convey very little about himself.

One day Mum and I came in to find Ian busy in my kitchen. My eyes met my mother's over his shoulder as he embraced me warmly and held me close. I could see how she was trying not to look shocked. There was her recently widowed daughter, devastated by her loss, actually enjoying the company of another man: a small, bespectacled man with curly blond hair, wearing Oxfam clothes and a pair of leather clogs, who had taken over the kitchen, shooing the children out, while he concocted delicious omelettes and crepes and served filtered coffee and dark chocolate biscuits. Another pair of his clogs were tucked neatly under a coffee table; his books, mostly classics and poetry, littering the top.

Our relationship was very intuitive. Ian could not be understood at a cerebral level, and most people tried then gave up. But his friendship was just what I needed – not to be analysed or told what to do, but just to be loved – with loving actions, a cup of coffee, a walk in the park, a meal with another friend, a glass of wine, someone to spend the evening with when the children had gone to bed. It was romantic in the purest sense, a true platonic friendship, so pure that he would even lie beside me when I'd gone to bed, like a friendly dog that senses his master is sad. And even on an occasion when we'd both had a bit too much wine, and had got somewhat maudlin over each other, he just could not take advantage of his very dear friend's trusting widow.

Sometimes we entertain the most unlikely angels unawares – and only God could have sent such a one to me. I adored him, even contemplated eventual marriage, but the thought never seemed to occur to him. I could sense that he loved very deeply, especially children, old people and animals, but knew well that he was not accepted by most people of his generation, because of his eccentricity. He was very physical and sensual – a huggy sort of person, who would wander around the house in his underpants without embarrassment. My friends would have been horrified, I knew, but it didn't bother me. In a sense he was just what I needed, filling the gap left by the physical absence of my departed husband yet not infringing the still-present sense of his spirit in the house. There was a bond of friendship too between Ian and Chris, a respect which had lasted from schooldays through the years when Ian was abroad, to the last few months of Chris's life. I sensed how much Ian cared for his friend, and also witnessed his very real grief at his death.

No one knew the hours we spent together. We were both 'morning' people, and I would often waken to hear him tiptoe up the stairs with a first cup of coffee. We thumbed our noses at polite Christian society, but we did not 'sin' in the usually accepted sense. A cynic would think it improbable, but yes, there can be life without sex between a caring man and woman, and we were blessed with a relationship that had more depth than can be found in most conventional marriages.

Ian introduced me to radio, and together we explored the wavebands, Radio 4 being the favourite. Television was opened up for me too, as we watched classics, comedy, word games and French cinema. But books were all-important, and as my new 'classics master' he introduced me to philosophy, psychology, The Jesuit, and classic stories such as The Leopard, The Little Prince and many more.

This all took place during the 1980s. Ian's visits became more difficult as the children became teenagers. They didn't appreciate his gifts of clothes from the Oxfam shop, and on occasions there was friction over the use of the telephone. He was not their father, as my daughter often informed him in anger. We drifted apart, and in 1993 he moved away.

I still have the letters he wrote to me when he was abroad with the British Council in Japan, Libya, Thailand and Indonesia, and also after he moved to Yorkshire where his family were living. They were full of chat about things he'd like me to read or listen to on the radio and reminiscences of our times together. Sadly they were not all dated, so I cannot put them in chronological order, but they are wonderful to re-read.

Ian continued to visit me in Holywood for many years after he moved to England, where his parents, brother and sister now lived. He also came with me to Donegal, where I had had caravan holidays with the children from 1982 until recently, and together we would explore the beautiful beaches, or he would take the older children climbing Mount Errigal while I stayed below with my youngest. On other occasions, he came to stay at my home, but the moment for togetherness had passed. I was trying to cope with teenage children as a single parent, and at times his presence made things awkward. On one occasion he borrowed my car and caused some damage at a roundabout, but would not reveal details to the insurance company. When pressed, he would become angry. I felt we were drifting apart.

And sadly, over the years Ian and I lost contact. My life moved on, I married again, but I often wondered if something had happened to him. However, through Facebook, I found an old school-friend of his sister, who put me in touch with the family, only to find that Ian had had a massive heart attack in 2010 or 2011. I grieved for his loss but was thankful for the happy times we had shared. He was a huge influence on me at a time in my life when I needed the sort of company he was able to provide. And I am eternally thankful that I chose not to 'toe the line' as a young widow coping in the Christian society I still belong to. He helped me to mature and grow in a way I might never have done had Chris still been alive.

There was an incident at the caravan at the end of the summer of 1987 that made me realise how I could appear vulnerable. We had a few really sunny days after a pretty wet season. Wishing to get as much benefit as possible from this last bit of sun, we donned our shorts and t-shirts. One teatime, there was no sign of Jonathan (aged six). I walked over to Paddy's Beach to find him, and happened to meet Derek P, who was seeing Paddy the site owner about getting some mastic for his van. He invited me to hop in and said he would give me a lift back to the caravan. I didn't think a lift was necessary, as it wasn't far and the weather was fine, but thinking he was just being friendly, I got in with Jonathan, me in the front and Jonathan in the back. On the way, the conversation turned to next year, and whether I would ever think of going somewhere hotter. I said I was happy with the little bit of sun we got at Melmore. Then somehow the conversation turned to my needs as a woman, and that it must be hard as a widow to have them met.

He enquired about whether I masturbated, and did I not feel the need for sex sometimes. I innocently said yes to both, but said I could wait until the right man turned up, though most men I met were already married. He went on to say he would always be available to me if I 'felt the need', and then his hand began to stray onto my bare legs, towards my shorts. And I think I just froze. At the same time, as a distraction he was showing Jonathan the 'amazing' way his Peugeot could be made to go up and down. We were now parked just in front of a friend's caravan near my own, and as his questions to me became more direct I just could not believe what was happening. My natural tendency is never to react suddenly, and I was so amazed that I think I just kept wondering what would happen next. But Jenny (then 15) appeared on the scene, it all stopped, and Jonathan and I got out.

Only when I was back in my own van making tea did I start to get quite angry about the whole thing, and a bit frightened about the implications. I decided we would go home first thing next day, and took care to lock my van door that night. I couldn't help muttering to Jenny about DP being a dirty old man, and when my friend Katherine from a neighbouring caravan came to see me about her mum Betty having gone home without her purse, I told her what had happened. She was not surprised, but very annoyed. Joe, her husband, was angry too. They both knew DP had a tendency to this sort of behaviour. Later DP came over 'to check my caravan for possible leaks', as if he were the first friend who had ever thought of helping me in a practical way. I was in such a turmoil that I couldn't bring myself to say anything, but I got rid of him as quickly as I could.

Next morning we left early, taking Betty's purse for her, and all the way home I was getting more and more angry and upset as I thought about the incident. I was in tears by the time we reached home. I let the kids in and said I had to take Betty's purse up to her. As soon as I got into Betty and Austin's house, I started crying and told Betty what had happened. She knew some of it already, as Katherine had been on the phone to her. I asked her advice and

Austin's, and they were very upset, and said I should tell John Ross, our minister, who was also a close friend of Derek's. I felt I couldn't talk to him about it, and Austin said he would phone him. I really dreaded having to speak to John about it, but realised it was the best thing to do.

Some days later, John came round and I had to tell him the details, though I couldn't bring myself to tell him all. He just said D tended to be an 'earthy sort', adding he was also the kindest and best friend he had, and so quick to help others. He said he would arrange to see D, and fix a time for the three of us to meet. Later, he brought Derek to see me. Derek said something about being in the 'dark night of the soul', and that was his excuse! And of course, nothing more was done. I felt guilty about not reporting him to a higher authority in the church for the sake of other people in a similar position. But I knew his wife, who was a lovely person, and I couldn't bring this hurt to her. I just hoped he did not try it with anyone else, especially younger people or teenagers, which he was rumoured to have done. Recently I decided to report the issue to the church after all. Now Derek has died, I hope it's over.

My 42nd birthday was approaching. Heather Harper CBE was retiring from a wonderful career as an operatic soprano, and was to be the star performer at a formal gala concert in the Ulster Hall on 17th March 1990. I really wanted to go, but there was no one to go with. Joe was a retired widower who had worked in the Air Force but had come back to his home town recently and joined the church of which I was a member. He was quite a bit older than me, but was dapper and young at heart, enjoyed music, and shared some other interests with me. So when he approached me asking if I had a long evening dress and would I like to go to the gala concert with him – well, what could I say! Yes, of course.

It was a wonderful evening, starting with a corsage and a taxi at the door, dinner at an intimate little restaurant in the city, chocolates at the interval and coffee afterwards. It was the start of a very pleasant friendship, which led on to something deeper. I was still relatively vulnerable, and although most of my friends, as well as my parents, advised against getting deeply involved with him, I was so in love with being in love again that I paid no attention to them. Joe was flamboyantly in love with me, and after a year or so went down on one knee in the back yard and asked me to marry him. By this time I was having second thoughts, and turned him down. Not wanting to hurt him, I tried to make sure we remained friends, but this became intolerable and I looked for some easy way to let him down lightly.

Then in 1991 someone else entered my life.

I was walking along the High Street when a car stopped at the traffic lights and a friendly voice asked 'What are you doing this summer?'

The man in the car was Chris's old pal and business partner, Richard. He stopped and we had a chat. He assured me he was now a 'recovering alcoholic'; he and his wife were separated; and he had been granted custody of their two children. I never really knew his wife, and he did not have a lot of good to say about her. But apparently, with the help of a good solicitor, he had won the case over custody. I could see that Richard loved his children, and they seemed happy to be with him. So I was interested to catch up with the family, and thought no more about it. In answer to his question I, perhaps foolishly, volunteered that we now had a caravan in Donegal and would be going there as soon as school was out. I thought nothing more of it until later that summer.

Once the school term was over, my three children and I headed off to our caravan. We lived a life of beach games, walking, barbecues, reading, board games, coffee with other caravan owners and sitting in the sun (when there was any). One fine day, while returning from a walk in the hills, there was an estate car on our plot, full of children and a dog. Of course, it was Richard's car. The children played, we had a meal, went for a walk, and I knew I was being courted. I liked him a lot, and it seemed the 'recovering alcoholic' status was still holding. Widowhood can be lonely, so this was indeed tempting.

Yes, I was being fairly naive, and it was foolish to invite him in, but I really thought I could be in control. He was a pleasant, affable type, and I badly needed some adult company. We took some short walks around the beautiful area of the headland at the caravan site. Alarm bells did begin to ring when he grabbed my hand and tried to kiss me, but by then I was enjoying the friendship too much. I made it clear that sex was not to be part of the relationship, but of course I didn't realise how vulnerable I was. He was great fun, an entrepreneur like Chris, always ready to help, and our children got on well together. The relationship was lively and yet intimate, and he seemed happy to compromise at a level of non-invasive sex. This satisfied my need for a physical relationship, and my conscience was reasonably clear. It was a Bill Clinton/Monica Lewinsky type of relationship.

After the holidays, Richard continued to visit. I found the relationship easy and satisfying and, as it went on, also exciting. Richard seemed well and truly shot of his earlier drinking habit. With the children now all at school, we would go off for the day to places like Benone beach near Limavady, where he had a dry cleaning business. One day he took me out for a drive in the mountains. We paused to look at the sunset. Richard turned to me, looked me in the eyes and stated, 'Some day I am going to marry you.' That was the nearest he ever got to a proposal; apart from anything else he wasn't divorced yet. However, we had fun days on the beach, and one day watched a ploughing competition. Back at home, he was very useful too, as he was able to fix things in the house and do any heavy work that was difficult for me. His elderly mother lived nearby in a council flat in the town, and we often visited her.

One day my mother said she was having a problem with her bathroom sink, and I suggested I had a friend who could have a look at it and could maybe fix the problem. So Richard was introduced as a 'friend'. But Mother was highly suspicious of his motives and went into defence mode regarding her widowed daughter. 'I think you're being very foolish!' she responded when I said he was 'just a friend'. That was his last visit to her home!

Richard owned or rented various seemingly tumbledown properties, or places in need of a lot of work, so in his usual jaunty fashion he found the children beds to sleep in at different places around the country. One of these was a disused gate-lodge. I don't think he paid any rent for it, but he had talked the owners into allowing him to use it if he looked after the property and did repairs. This he did with great zeal, and it became a secret little hideaway for us.

When my daughter Jenny finished her time at the local school, coming out with reasonably good A-levels, she eventually got a place at Manchester Metropolitan University. Jenny disappeared off to Spain with her friends as soon as she knew she had passed her exams, leaving me to find her accommodation in Manchester. Unfortunately, by the time I made contact with the university, the standard halls of residence were all full. After much searching and phoning around, a room was found unseen.

Richard accompanied us across in the boat to Stranraer. We drove down through England through the night, stopping to sleep in the car at motorway service stations. We arrived in Manchester bedraggled and tired and asked to see the owner of Jenny's room, who was known as Mr Ali. Mr Ali showed us the room and kitchen we had chosen. It was at the top of the house, and Richard enquired where the fire escape was. 'You call the fire brigade and they lift you down,' said Mr Ali. The kitchen cookware and surfaces were covered with a layer of grease. Together we set about making it more presentable and suitable for use.

Later, as the younger children were getting on well, Richard and I thought about a holiday together. I had been looking at Christian single parent holidays, and found one in Wales. We would be camping beside the River Wye, and canoeing was on the programme. By then Jenny was away at uni, so we packed Richard's scruffy estate car with our tent, clothing and sleeping bags and set off with my two boys and Richard's son and daughter. It was a beautiful spot, the weather was good, and we loved the whole sense of adventure. As the holiday was run by a charity, food was supplied in the form of Marks and Spencer end-of-day leftovers, and they were really appreciated after long days out of doors, on and in the water.

Over the years since his marriage, Richard had collected together lots of pieces of furniture and fittings he planned to use wherever he settled down, but often he did not have room for them and they ended up in my spacious terraced house. One of these was a large chandelier, which he proceeded to fit in my hallway. I liked it and it added to the Victorian character of the terrace.

Richard had been an alcoholic until fairly recently. He had in fact reached a point of alcohol abuse where he realised if he went on he would kill himself. But at his very lowest ebb, he said 'a higher power' took control, and from that moment he never touched another drop. I told him only God could have done that, and he became interested in Christianity and even came to church with me quite often. This helped me justify our friendship to myself.

However, this relationship was not to last. It eventually broke down for several reasons. His personality was such that he became possessive of me. He was also easily annoyed by chance remarks that I made without realising he might perceive them as hurtful. Instead of talking about it, he would just walk out of the room, leaving me wondering what it was I had said to upset him. I began to feel that things were getting out of hand, and tried to end the relationship a couple of times.

Richard would not accept this. The final straw for him was when, after telling him I was finishing it, I put an advertisement in the personal column of the local newspaper to find another more suitable friend, this time with a view to marriage. And I arranged to meet the person who answered.

Richard became extremely angry, and without speaking came to the house to collect anything that was his, including the chandelier in the hallway. The day he came to collect it, he was in a really rough mood. He was very angry that I had ditched him for someone else. Refusing to speak, he set about single-handedly removing the chandelier. This involved lifting the floorboards of the landing above. Fortunately, my son Niall was at home at the time, so I felt reasonably safe in spite of Richard's silent angry mood. Niall offered to help and this was refused. I offered a coffee and it was also refused. When I made it anyway and set it beside him on the floor, it was ignored, though he must have been thirsty.

I reassured myself that this was the last time Richard would need to take anything from the house, and I hoped it would be the last I saw of him, as I had started meeting the new man in my life, John.

However, for the next few months, Richard became a stalker. He put notes through my door, repeatedly drove past the house and phoned so often that I had to install an answering machine to identify who was calling before I answered.

Other incidents were occurring that worried me a lot. I had been taking lodgers to help increase my income as I was not yet working again, and at that time there were a couple of Spanish girls staying upstairs in the room that used to be Jenny's. One of them reported to me that some of her underwear had gone missing. I searched everywhere but could not find it. I also noticed that some of my own underwear was also missing, until one day I noticed some of it stuck down behind a radiator in the bedroom.

But the Spanish girls were still missing items. I began to search more urgently, as I was beginning to suspect Richard might be involved. The house, of course, was always locked when we were out, but it occurred to me that the bathroom window gave onto the roof of the outhouses below, and it was not locked nor did it have a key. The only person who knew this, apart from myself and my family, was Richard. So I started looking in other places only Richard would be aware of. Remembering the chandelier, I lifted the floorboards in the landing above the hallway, and there we found a collection of knickers and bras. Then other possible hiding places occurred to me. While lying in the bath one evening, I remembered that Richard had taken off the bath panel at one time to fix a leak. Removing the panel, there we found more underwear. It seemed that this was his way of getting back at me for dumping him. At least, I thought, he was not keeping the underwear for bizarre purposes, except that my favourite black bra never turned up!

I began to feel quite scared. I was starting to have nightmares, and in one of them I dreamt I was answering a call at the front door. On opening it I was met with a man with a gun. Bizarre, yes, and very scary! When an opportunity came to attend a counselling session on fear, I gratefully accepted it. At this point I decided to contact the police. They asked whether I wanted to make a complaint, and if so they would speak to Richard. But I thought this might just make things worse for me, so I said no. Gradually I came to terms with the fear. I tried to forget about him and hoped the stalking would cease, which it eventually did. And one day I was inspired to write a poem, actually a limerick, about the incident, and it made me laugh so much every time I read it that my fear disappeared.

These days I sometimes see Richard in the town and he is friendly. There is no mention of the past. He found another girlfriend. And some day, I will give him a copy of the limerick I wrote:

> *There was once an inventor called Richard*
> *Who devised a machine to make knickers*
> *But the machine had a curse!*
> *It went in reverse!!*
> *And he had to feed its voracious appetite with all the ladies underwear he could lay his hands on!!!!*

How do you sum up, looking back, a relationship that lasted 14 years but in the end just didn't work?

I had just decided to come out of a quite terrifying relationship with Richard (the sixth relationship overall, of which three were truly beautiful, though each in a different way). This time I went for the personal column option for the very first time. (These were the days before internet dating.)

My first attempts were not very successful. I would forget to put height as a requirement and find myself on a date with someone a head shorter than me. Or they would turn out to be boring or scruffy or a Mummy's boy. Then, in 1993, a good friend living in England came to visit and we had a girls' night out. She decided to take me in hand and we scoured the paper for a suitable man looking for someone special. Over the years I had decided that single men of my age were perhaps too set in their ways to become married, while divorced or separated ones brought too much previous baggage with them. This left widowers, and it seemed that most of them remarried quite quickly. It was a case of catching one before someone else did!

We discovered a widower looking for a 'tall attractive widow' and I responded to the box number, giving brief details about myself and my telephone number. Sometime later I received a long letter addressed to BT Subscriber No. XXXXXX, followed by my address. Before trying to work out how a letter had reached me via this strange means, I read the letter. Its writer seemed really nice, too good to be true almost: six foot six tall, lived locally, belonged to a local Presbyterian church. He sounded just right for me, though who can really tell at this stage of a relationship?

The letter-writer told me how he had just lost his wife to a mysterious blood disorder, which of course interested me as a nurse and also because Chris had died of leukaemia. He had two daughters still at school, and seemed to be a bit of an entrepreneur with his own business. This too made him sound quite similar to Chris. So we agreed to meet up at a nearby restaurant, as he lived within a few miles of my home. I discovered he belonged to a local Presbyterian church and to Mensa, the organisation for brainy people. He liked doing puzzles and competitions, and had in fact had a really big win – a totally ecologically built house in a nearby town. Yet more similarity, as Chris had been very interested in energy saving projects.

Now you might wonder how he knew what address to send the letter to as, even back then, privacy was considered important especially in the personal column, where box numbers were provided. By an ingenious method, which I have to say impressed me, he had got my address from BT just by giving them my telephone number, which was not ex-directory! As by now you might realise, I am not a highly suspicious person but have more of a trusting nature, and yeah, looking back, maybe I should have been more suspicious.

His name was John, he was tall and rather handsome, and he had an English accent, as he had been born and raised in Kent. His father was English and his mother was from Northern Ireland. They had divorced some years before (his father having gone off with his secretary) and John had moved to Northern Ireland to be near his mother when he went to university. I noticed that I seemed to prefer men who had not been totally absorbed in the Northern Irish scene all their lives – although Chris was from Northern Ireland, his parents had travelled – and an English accent seemed to me a great asset.

At the beginning, John took me to see the new house he had won in the competition. He told me he had another house in the country, but was in the process of deciding what to do about the problem of now having two homes. The country house where John lived had been a labourers' abandoned cottage, which he and his wife had bought cheaply and made the way they wanted it. It had a large garden, and John had planted the front area with many unusual flowers, shrubs and plants. At the back he had a greenhouse and a large fruit and vegetable area. Inside, the house was more or less just as his wife had left it, a little bit old-fashioned, full of her books, and the wallpaper was starting to look a bit grey.

I found John utterly charming, and before long we had become 'an item'. However, his mother-in-law was not happy that he was seeing someone else so soon after his wife had died, so I didn't meet that side of the family for quite some time.

For a time I got on well with his two daughters, who were younger than my own children and were still at school. They of course missed their mother terribly. In due course, I was taken to see John's house in the country, and eventually he decided to sell the house he had won, so it seemed that financially he was in a pretty good position. Over the 14 years we were together, we never moved in together, but stayed in each other's house as it suited us; for example, I would stay over on the days when it would be helpful for me to take John's girls to school. He didn't seem interested in making any changes to his house, even to redecorate, so after a while I stopped suggesting it. I thought he just needed time before he would be able to truly move on from his wife's death.

In summer, we went to my caravan in Donegal, which John and his girls loved. Being such a practical sort of man, he was of great help there. Soon we decided to upgrade together to a much larger caravan on the same site as the previous van, which was by now on its last legs. The site had no street lights, electricity or sewerage system, but like everyone else on the site we preferred it that way, for many reasons – such as not having to share toilets or showers, being able to see the stars at night and, of course, paying less rent. We had been using a flimsy nylon toilet tent, and the first thing John did was to build a wooden shed behind the caravan, which would also house things like tools or wetsuits. On its roof he fixed a solar panel and attached it to a pair of large car batteries, which would store the electricity gathered from the panel. This was then used to power some electric lights and to pump water to the kitchen taps in the van. Previously, we had had to go with 20-litre plastic water bottles to one of the taps on the site and lug them back to the caravan. So now, you ask, where would the water come from? We had also had a water butt at one corner outside the van, linked by pipes to the tiny water channels on the roof, to use for cooking and washing. The water coming off the roof was just rainwater, and was quite clean and unpolluted on this part of the Donegal coast (apart from the odd seagull dropping). It was wonderful for washing hair as it was so soft, also for washing dishes, cooking and even drinking when boiled. So the next stage was to get a much larger water container, which could be connected to the pump and the taps. Full of ideas, John purchased a brand new 300-gallon oil tank. Before the new caravan was installed on site, he had a large pit dug in the sand below the position where the pump was to go. He set the tank and the pump in place and connected the pipes to the water taps. Running water at last! This was a wonderful improvement on our previous arrangement.

We used to bring our cat on holiday, and she liked to go hunting. She would catch baby rabbits and take them under the van at night. We would hear their cries and in the morning find nothing left but their little white tails.

John had purchased a small boat recently, and before long he decided to take it up to the caravan site in Donegal. He had bought it cheaply along with a boat trailer, as someone had towed it down a motorway not realising that the boat was scraping along the road surface and had developed a hole. Being made of fibreglass, it was easy enough to repair, so for the next few summers we had a means of catching the local fish – mackerel, mainly, but also pollock, skate, dabs and dogfish. Also, we found a second-hand lobster pot, placed it deep in the sea near the headland, and had a fair catch every year of edible crabs and lobsters. We threw them in the pot and boiled them, then learned how to remove the flesh for delicious meals. The cat loved the smell of crabs being prepared outside on the picnic table.

Never having had much experience in small boats before, I took to the new experience with a certain sense of excitement. I preferred tranquil days when the sun shone and the sea was calm and we could sunbathe on deck, rather than the choppy moments when the wind would suddenly spring up, and toss us about in our little vessel. Out of season, we moored it behind the house of the site owner, then in early summer took it to a small bay at the head of the lough. We would launch the boat with the help of the children, test the engine, then push the throttle up and head for the bay near the caravan. Here it was moored with a small anchor. We also acquired a tiny folding vessel, strangely similar to an umbrella, as a tender to reach the boat at the beginning and end of the season. On a good day, we would head across the mouth of the lough and land on the further shore to explore the area that we could otherwise see only from a distance. It was like landing on a foreign shore, as we had never been there by car, and to reach it by road would have meant a journey of a couple of hours.

Back home, as our friendship developed, I tried to think of a way to meet John's in-laws. There was his elderly mother-in-law, who apparently disapproved strongly of me, and his two sisters-in-law. I got to know one quite well. When John dropped off his daughters for a visit to their granny, he had to park the car a distance from her house, so that she would not see me! However, I eventually thought of a way to meet the mother-in-law and show that I was really not a monster. I invited her to my house for a proper Sunday dinner (John and his girls had always gone to her for Sunday dinner), and from then on the relationship improved and I started to be accepted.

Later, we visited John's family in England, including his sister, who had just been diagnosed with lung cancer and who died some years later. We also booked holidays abroad: to Guernsey (where John had worked as a student, picking fruit), Lanzarote, Tunisia, Portugal and Morocco. I felt we had become a couple, and would have been happy to marry him, but he never asked me. Looking at rings on holiday one time, John said he would be happy to buy me one, so long as I didn't attach any significance to it! I told myself to simply enjoy his friendship and not expect anything more. After all, in this modern world there was really no need to get married for two people who each already had their own children.

John and I went to some memorable parties. On 17th March 2000, it was my birthday, and St Patrick's Day to boot. That evening, we set out with our friends John and Anne to a formal party at Castle Ellen, near Athenry in Co Galway. Being unfamiliar with the area, we drove through Athenry village, and out under one of the arches. We tried various long driveways from the road and at last we came upon a sign for Castle Ellen, pointing back the way we had come!! Performing a difficult U-turn, we confused other traffic also doing U-turns, and finally reached an entrance on the left, which had a sign bedecked with the Irish army flag. The gateway itself was hardly wide enough to allow our modest saloon through. We proceeded up the grassy driveway for about a quarter of a mile until we came upon the house itself, transcendent in moonlight.

The host was Chief Engineer with Galway Council and had bought the property in a state of great disrepair. He was welcoming guests in army uniforms with their lady companions, who wore long velvet capes to protect them from the still, cool evening air. We joined them ascending the wide stone steps, which rose directly from the grassy frontage. In the dim moonlight, while our eyes adjusted to the poor electric lighting (30 watts having been the maximum permitted when such lighting was a novelty), the entrance was a picture of decadence.

144

A stuffed red fox gazed at us through a mask from some long-forgotten masked ball. Rotting flags of old regiments, and branches still holding their dried autumn leaves, adorned the walls. Brown sacking held together crumbling parts of the old coving above the front door. Inside, doorways on left and right gave glimpses through new plate-glass panels of bare pinewood floors with occasional pieces of old furniture and marble fireplaces. Military music played as we were welcomed and ushered past the old staircase, which rose centrally but ended mid-air at the top of the first flight. More stuffed animals observed us from various levels of the staircase. In the Long Room on the right a blazing log fire threw flickering shadows around the walls, and guests helped themselves from the makeshift bar in the corner. Old pews and pine benches provided some seating, though the guests stood mostly in groups by the fire or near the uncurtained windows. A pair of stone peafowl faced out to the estate on either side of the bay window, and a Corinthian column supported a stucco objet d'art in the central window. The wall opposite the fire was painted cream. The other walls were dark red, and an ancient torn paper Christmas star, bedecked with gold paint, inadequately screened a 20-watt central light bulb. As we chatted, more guests arrived: an Irish army chief in his moss-green uniform, and a bearded redcoat sporting a long sword.

We were invited to cross the hallway and help ourselves to the banquet spread out on the T-shaped table, which extended through two rooms. These were warmed by blazing log fires. A dearth of sharp knives led to the redcoat offering to carve a whole chicken with his épée, to the amazement of the ladies. After dinner, speeches were made in English followed by Irish, which somehow seemed the natural tongue in this old Irish house, wreathed in history. It had once been the family home of the ancestors of Lord Edward Carson, whose mother was Isabella Lambert.

So John and I passed several happy years together. But the relationship started to go stale. I noticed he was becoming less attentive to me. Physical affection was undeniably dwindling. I wrote in my diary on 6th August 2006: 'Situation becoming clearer. The problem is that I am a person of passion and he is a cold fish, or has become one. I have spent the last three years trying to relight the dying embers of his fire. What does he get passionate about?'

At one point I suggested to him that we might break up, as he didn't seem as keen to continue the relationship as I was. To my surprise his eyes filled with tears. In some ways he was a very inhibited type, and I supposed at the time that he just had difficulty expressing his feelings.

Eventually I asked him to marry me. No reply. Had he tired of me? Or perhaps there was another reason – another woman? I asked straight out: 'Are you seeing someone else?' He responded, 'No, of course not!'

I left it at that for the time being. The following July we headed north again, John at the wheel, the children in the back, older now but still looking forward to the freedom of Donegal. I told myself I was reasonably content with my life, even though I would have liked to get married. Unexpectedly, I felt tears welling up as we left the motorway for the narrower country roads. Perhaps it was because when I had questioned John again recently, he had suggested that maybe we were now more like brother and sister. This was not indeed the relationship I had in mind! Embarrassed now that the children might have noticed my tears, I made a joke of it, remembering reading somewhere that menopause often caused this type of mood for no reason.

The moment passed, and the summer weeks were as usual filled with boating, fishing, barbecuing, sunbathing and sightseeing. At the end of July we went home to restock with food supplies and harvest

146

the fruit from John's back garden. He and I planned to go back to the caravan the following weekend. It would be just the two of us as the children were now old enough to stay home alone or with friends for a few days. I had booked a table at our favourite Italian restaurant in Letterkenny, and was looking forward to some quality time with him. His birthday was in August, and I had bought him a new lobster pot, which he would find when we returned to the van. The day before we left, I went up to his house to deliver his birthday card.

As I drove into the back yard, I noticed another car parked by the back door. As there was no sign of anyone in the kitchen, I wandered out to the garden where he might be picking raspberries or peas. Ah yes, there was a visitor that I didn't recognise, and he was showing her around the garden, coffee cups in hand. 'Is there a cup of coffee going?' I casually enquired, and we entered the kitchen again to put the kettle on. But as we chatted, there was something in this lady's demeanour that worried me. I had never seen her before and she was just introduced as 'Margaret'. She busied herself making coffee, and then settled herself comfortably at the kitchen table, while I had to stand near the door. I was starting to feel nervous.

I felt I needed to explain. 'John and I are off in the morning to Donegal for the weekend – it's his birthday tomorrow. His present is there already, but I just called in to give him his card. We'll leave mid-afternoon, and stop off at our favourite restaurant in Letterkenny for a pizza on the way.' There was an awkward pause, and I started to wonder what exactly was going on. In my nervousness, I spilled my coffee, but Margaret was quick to jump up and find a cloth, wiping up the mess before settling herself once more at the table. 'She's acting like it's her own house,' I thought, getting more and more concerned. I was beginning to feel like I was on a stage taking part in a drama, but decided to play along with it and see how it would end.

Next day, as planned, John and I set off for Donegal. On the journey, no mention was made of the incident of the previous evening. We were just pleasantly enjoying the trip, and talking about what we would do when we arrived. I waited for him to bring up the subject, but was somewhat disappointed when no mention was made.

The restaurant was crowded and noisy, full of families with children. We found a table, chose our pizzas, and as we waited for them to arrive, I took a deep breath and asked, 'So who is Margaret?'

'Oh, just a friend....' John said vaguely. And from there the mood suddenly changed.

'You must think I am completely stupid!' I bawled. Tears began to well up as I spoke. I glanced over my shoulder at the families around us, who were suddenly interested in this respectable, well-dressed couple, who had seemed so cool and in control when first entering the restaurant. Forks poised midair. Everyone was looking at us. In icy tones I made it clear that I was not to be messed with. But as my questions continued and my companion tried to wriggle out of answering them, my voice was rising. Suddenly emotion took over, tears flew and the handsome man looked like he wished the floor would open! Amid stony silence we finished our pizzas and left for the car.

The rest of the journey was not quite so dramatic. In fact we didn't speak until we reached the caravan site. On arrival, we each busied ourselves with practicalities without speaking a word. John settled himself on one of the narrow bunks for the night, and somehow we managed to pass the days until it was time to leave for home.

And so ended a promising friendship, one that had lasted 14 years. I slowly came to terms with the situation, and in retrospect came to the conclusion, sadly, that there had never been any love in the relationship: it was just a practical arrangement. John, to my mind, was a complete rat, in that he had never been able to talk about how he felt, and had actually used a dating site to find a replacement for me before even saying he was not happy. It turned out later that he had brought Margaret to the caravan for a weekend, introducing her to other caravanners as 'sister'. He and Margaret soon married, but I really didn't care anymore.

Next July, I went alone to my caravan at Melmore. This was the first long stretch I had spent there since John left, and it was hard enough. I busied myself on my laptop and kept typing up my diary entries to be copy-pasted in later. One Monday I tried the Wi-Fi hotspot we had found the previous year at the Rosapenna Hotel, and got as far as reading emails, but it was a very poor connection and kept cutting out. I tried again the following night and it wouldn't work at all. But one night I'd been to see Talking Through His Hat at the Errigal Arts Festival – 'An Encounter with Jonathan Swift'. On the way back I kept trying to sign in all the way between Dunfanaghy and the caravan site, and at last found a great connection at the Beach Hotel in Downings.

So far only a day and a half out of six had been wet, and I had been sunbathing and reading most of the time, chatting with friends, walking on the beach. My old school chum Janet came over on Thursday and we had a long walk and, later on, had a BBQ. I'd also been through the cupboards and under the beds, and had filled a black bag with things of John's as I preferred not to be reminded of him: old boat shoes, blankets and sleeping bags belonging to his girls, a tin of steak and kidney pie (one of his special favourites), a cushion knitted by his mother-in-law, an old brass shell he had found when using the metal-detector I gave him for a birthday (what fun we had with that!). I wondered about including the crab and lobster shells that decorated the shelf above the windows, which he was so proud of and so enjoyed catching in his lobster pot. But how to get his stuff back to him? I didn't want to drive up to his house and possibly meet him (or her!) on the doorstep as I was trying to sneak away. Maybe I'd ask a friend to do it...

That black bag was also delivering a strong message: I want to put you right out of my life. Harder said than done as I sat in the place where we had so often sat and read together and played Scrabble so companionably. I was so glad to have several good friends around in other caravans who understood and had invited me for coffee and meals with them, but sometimes I just felt desperately lonely. I was so used to being in companionship with someone: 14 years with John; a year or two with two other guys; before that the children were all at home; and before that almost 14 years with Chris. I took a walk along the empty beach that night, feeling tearful, and sat at the end of the bay full of emotion.

Looking along the beach, I noticed a man on his own walking in my direction, so I jumped up and climbed up to the road, thinking I wouldn't be able to even say Hi in my state. He looked lonely, as if he had lost someone as well, but he stopped to talk to another man. I thought maybe I could contrive a meeting some way so that we could chat.

However, while I was missing John, my loss was nothing compared to the tragedy that had recently stricken my brother Arthur's side of the family. Several months earlier, Arthur had phoned to tell me he had just taken his daughter Lindsay to their local hospital – they lived in Banbridge, Co Down – as she had come back from a trip to Africa with severe headaches. Lindsay was the third of Arthur's four children, exceptionally beautiful and deeply interested in third-world charity work. She had just married her fiancé Alain, and they were looking forward to starting work together for a charity in Africa. The hospital that night delivered the dreadful news that Lindsay had a brain tumour. Operations and treatments followed, but within months – in April 2007 – Lindsay died, aged just 23. It was a dreadful time for our whole family, especially her husband Alain and her mother Liz.

Alain wrote every day in a blog, expressing his grief so eloquently, and I found it good to read and share his feelings. Alone at Melmore, I carried on reading his blog, and was deeply impressed with how he was coming to terms with Lin's death. It was good to have my brother Arthur here the weekend before I came for the long break, and he texted to say he enjoyed it too. This is a place where it's easy to think things through, cry, think, adjust, re-adjust... I think he found that. I just hoped Liz would find somewhere she could do that too. I didn't think Melmore was the place for her; it's not for everyone.

But it comforted me the way it had always done. Here are three poems I wrote about staying in our caravan in Donegal.

COMING BACK TO DONEGAL

Family connections drew us to the place
And, freshly united at our marriage vows,
We set out to explore the places we had known,
And re-discover for ourselves
Atlantic Drive, The Rosses, Bloody Foreland
And Horn Head.

Later, with carrycot in back,
The pure sand drew us to its shores,
And little fingers searched for shells.

Thatched   cottages   in   agents'   windows
Caught our imagination, planned retreats in back of beyond,
Away from telephones and urgent calls.

It   was   our   place.
Yes, there were rows, as tensions were released -
Which   way   to   go —
Children   behaving   badly   in   hotels,
Pyjama'd   figures   in   formal   dining   rooms.
The   usual   family   strife.
Expectations   of   holiday   bliss
Shattered by toddlers in strange bedrooms.

Now   husbandless   and   fatherless
It   draws   us   back.
Wild   headlands,   deserted   beaches,
Sou'westered   walks   in   drizzle,
Sunny   days   on   sand.
The   wild   beauty   of   the   Downings,
Atlantic Drive and Dooey village.

Climbing   up   the   road   to   look
Back   down   at   Trannarossan,
Precious   memories   catch   my   throat.
I   revel   in   its   pathos,
Remembering   how   we   stopped
To   stroke   a   donkey,

The   children   lifting   grass   on
Palm of hand. We do it once again.

He   is   not   there   in   body,
But   I   sense   his   spirit   watching,
Keeping   step   with   us –
His   place.   Our   place.
Except   for   Melmore,   which   is   ours,
Not   his.
A   new   life   starts.   The   past   was   good.
The   present   also.   The   future   lies
With God – and He is good.

CARAVAN

A   pile   of   books   selected   at   the   busy   time   of   year
For   languid   days   with   feet   up   on   the   bunk.
A   board   game   started   back   at   Easter,
Dusted with a light scattering of sand.

In   our   little   hollow   we   can   see   the   waves
break   on   the   north   beach.
Not   much   else.   Some   lazy   cows
butting   each   other   as   they   trundle   home.
But,   down   the   path,   the   biggest   beach   extends
towards   the   lighthouse   and   the   tip   of   Melmore   Head
And boats in the bay of every size.

This is the place where ecstasy resides.
In rain or sunny days it matters not.
We go to rest
and find again our peace.
No telephone or plans to carry through.
A place to fill our souls
with God's own country.

DONEGAL

I walked along the sand at Paddy's Beach,
The children fast asleep in the four-berth van.

I climbed a cliff at the Murderhole Beach,
Leaned back against the hardness of the granite wall,
And watched them dare the waves to wet their feet.

And God and Nature folded me within their arms.

I felt alone and yet content. Pathos and joy.

I sensed I was a part of something greater –
His greatness, my insignificance.

To think that in His plan there was a place for me...

> *I   gave   myself   to   Him   again,*
> *And felt at one with Him and Nature and the world.*

Downsizing to a new apartment at Lesley Mews in February 2000

Out and about at Donaghadee with Lynn Stratton

With friends Nigel Kingsley, Bob Ballagh, Jonathan and John Rickard

Ian MacDonald with Jonathan

Enjoying the social scene again with my friend Joe Pomeroy

On holiday with the boys and Lynn in Cyprus

6

A NEW BEGINNING

Ilt was my second cousin Lynn who introduced me to Paul. But in

sowing the seeds of a new relationship, she also brought about the
end of her longstanding friendship with me.

Lynn and I had been quite close during our nurse training days,
and she had been a bridesmaid at my wedding. After qualifying, she
had gone to work as the matron of a boys' boarding school in West
Sussex. Here she fell in love with one of the masters and they
married in 1980. Her husband Keith was a committed Christian,
which pleased Lynn's parents, and together they attended the local
Baptist church. She had problems with some of her pregnancies,
which sadly ended in miscarriage, but her son Mark was born around
the same time as my Jonathan. The boys became good friends, and
drew us closer together. When Chris died, Lynn stayed with me for a
few nights and was a great support to me.

Keith did not enjoy beach holidays in hot places, so over the years
my cousin and I shared several trips to Cyprus with our children.
The holidays were a great success, especially as Niall was old
enough to babysit the children on occasion while Lynn and I went
out for dinner.

Sadly, Keith fell ill with Hodgkin's disease, and subsequently
died. Now it was my turn to support my cousin, and as widows we
became more and more like sisters. We started taking an interest in

male friendships again. But our experiences ended messily, so we found ourselves sharing our sadness once more.

Around this time, Lynn's parents went into residential care near my home, and she stayed with me whenever she came to see them. When her father asked, 'Where are you staying?' she would say, 'With Norah', and he would nod, 'That's good.' After her mother died, she came more often to visit him, and our friendship went on maturing. When the time came for Lynn's son Mark to marry, I was invited to the wedding in England. Lynn met me at the airport, took me to the hotel where accommodation was to be provided in log cabins for the weekend, and introduced me to the family of Becky, the bride. One of them – her new daughter-in-law's grandfather Paul – she confided, 'might be a catch'. One day Paul asked me to go with him to the nearby town to buy a paper and have a coffee. Never looking a gift-horse in the mouth, I went. Lynn made clear she wasn't interested in Paul. Paul and I got on fine, but apart from exchanging a few emails in the next week or two, that was as far as it went.

Paul was a retired engineer from Hampshire. Born in 1936 in London to Dorothy and Edward Davis, he had been educated at Wimbledon and had begun his career as a senior aircraft manager with the RAF on National Service and had gone on to specialise in electrical and electronic engineering. He became a planning engineer with Ronson and Plessey and later started his own business in bespoke furniture manufacture. His marriage to his first wife, Julie, had ended in 1972 and his three grown-up children, Lindy, Karen and Stephen now lived in the USA, Canada and Australia respectively with their spouses and children.

Like me, Paul loved travelling. He had visited India, Nigeria, North and South America, Australia, Canada, China and the Galapagos Islands, and had lived for a time on the Isle of Wight, where he could indulge his love of sailing. He and I also shared a love for books, poetry and philosophy, and we discovered we had similar tastes in music, starting with a Jake Thackray CD we each happened to own. Paul had a huge collection of CDs, and other joint favourites were Van Morrison, Eric Clapton and Julian Lloyd Webber. An old song we specially loved, and later became strangely appropriate, was Plaisir d'Amour (Sweet Joys of Love), which starts and ends:

'Sweet joys of love are here but for a while; like blissful dreams they are gone with the morning.'

About three years after Mark and Becky's wedding, Paul asked if I'd be in England again soon. As it happened I was about to visit my daughter in London, and agreed to meet him for lunch. It went well. I wasn't sure where it might lead, but I felt more comfortable with Paul, who was 10 years older than me and almost a family member, than with some of the internet dates I had tried.

Paul, however, seemed completely sure where it would lead. Three emails later, he declared his love by email in no uncertain terms. 'Down, dog!' I replied. 'You couldn't possibly love me. You hardly know me. And I have lots of horrible habits!' Undeterred, Paul came to visit me in Ireland.

Next time Lynn came to stay while visiting her father, she asked whether I had got any sort of relationship going with Paul. Not being sure myself, I rather brushed off the question. I thought nothing more of the matter until some time later when she accused me of hiding things from her. She thought I had been meeting up with Paul without telling her. I strongly denied it, but she didn't believe me.

I thought the spat would blow over. When I started seeing more of Paul and even going on holiday with him, I sent Lynn postcards of where we were staying. But the response was a succession of angry emails. I couldn't understand it. Perhaps Lynn felt our lives had mirrored each other's so closely that if one took a different path, the other had the right to feel abandoned. I kept writing to her, but she declared she never wanted to hear from me again. When Paul and I eventually married, we didn't invite Lynn. Mark and Becky came to the wedding but they did not stay for the reception. One last attempt to contact Lynn through a mutual relative resulted in a phone call to say we had nothing in common any more. And so ended a good friendship for seemingly no good reason.

For my part, the relationship with Paul grew over years rather than weeks. We travelled back and forth between England and Ireland, and took a few holidays together. The first was to Cornwall in 2009, when Paul chose a beautiful though quite expensive B&B and we explored the Eden Project and Tintagel.

Eventually, Paul proposed. I did waver for a while. Several events led me to suspect he could be a candidate for Alzheimer's. Once while staying at his flat, I found him in the living room in the middle of the night, not knowing what time or day it was.

I had already had some involvement with people with Alzheimer's. The first had been my mother-in-law Lilla. A very independent lady since her husband Harry had died, Lilla had taught in the local primary school and loved helping her grandchildren with their reading. But as Alzheimer's took hold, her driving became erratic and I was often called to help her if she became lost or could not turn her car in a street. Later, she became unable to recognise people she knew like myself, saying, 'my daughter-in-law gave me this!' Or she would be found crossing a road early in the morning, saying she had been asked to help with teaching in a school, and was getting the bus there. Eventually she went into care at a series of nursing homes, where I became responsible for her care as her other son was living in Dublin. She died unable to swallow.

So I was aware that Alzheimer's, if confirmed in Paul, would be progressive and irreversible, and I thought about breaking up with him. But he was so lovely and, at that stage, such events were few and far between. And as a nurse, I was used to the practical side of caring for people.

I talked to my daughter and a couple of friends about my feelings for Paul, and in the end decided, 'I can do this!' We set a date for May 2010.

We were married in a beautiful little Elizabethan church called Old St Peter's in Stockbridge, Hampshire. The church been founded in the twelfth century and restored in Tudor times. Its original chancel had fallen into disrepair by 1863 but had been renovated in 1963, along with an old ochre mural to Elizabeth I on an interior wall of the building. So I thought it would be fitting to enter the church to the music of 'Greensleeves', with Paul's daughter Lindy on guitar and Jenny's mother-in-law Marg on flute. We had Jenny as matron of honour and her two-month-old daughter Imogen as bridesmaid. At the ceremony this poem, an Apache prayer, was read:

> *Now you will feel no rain, for each of you will be shelter for the   other.*
> *Now you will feel no cold, for each of you will be warmth to the   other.*
> *Now there is no loneliness for you: now you are two persons,*
> *But   there   is   only   one   life   before   you.*
> *Go now to your dwelling place, to enter into the days of your togetherness,*
> *And may your days be good and long together.*

Over the 10 years we were together, we managed to fit in quite a lot! My first marriage had been love at first sight and lasted just 14 years. Paul was also the love you always would have dreamed of. Coming together was our Karma. We were indeed soul mates – music lovers, avid book-readers, poetry addicts, and we also liked to travel. At the end of each day, we often read to each other in bed: some of the books we had enjoyed, and poetry that spoke to our heart. Karma meant we often discovered books we each had read, and which mentioned places we each had hoped to visit, like Pompeii. So together we visited Italy and fulfilled that desire together. We never stopped caring for each other. Even after he developed Alzheimer's, and well after it reached a stage where I could not manage his care myself, he still always said, 'It's lovely to see you,' and showed love in whatever ways he could.

Following our wedding, we took a few days' honeymoon at my caravan in Donegal. Sadly, this didn't work out well, as Paul found it unsettling to wake at night in the dark and find himself in unfamiliar surroundings.

We decided to sell both his flat and mine and buy a bungalow in Holywood. But in the middle of the negotiations, I contracted TB due to the side-effects of my rheumatoid arthritis medication, and had to spend a month in hospital. Paul took over all the arrangements for the house purchase and still managed to visit me every day. It was lovely to feel I had someone to look after me and no paperwork to worry about. Soon after I got home, he built new doors and a wardrobe, chose oak flooring and got it laid, and tiled the kitchen walls.

But this comfortable state of mind could not last. Paul had obtained a quote of £1,100 for removal of his flat contents to Holywood, and a date was arranged for August 2010. However, he forgot which date it was, and when they arrived to take the contents he was nowhere near ready. They charged him about £1,000 to re-arrange the move.

On the day we were moving, I was driving. Relying on Paul to keep the timings right, I assumed we could allow ourselves to enjoy the journey. Having stopped for lunch and taken time to admire the scenery, we arrived at the dock to find the boat had gone. And we had to pay the fare again for the next boat, which arrived in Dublin in the middle of the night, after which we had to drive the 100 miles to Holywood in time to meet the removal team and van. We only just made it!

Paul and I shared many happy times. We had some memorable holidays together. We took a trip to Paris, where my son was living at the time, and another to Italy to see Mount Vesuvius. In 2012 we visited Paul's daughter Lindy in Michigan, and the following year Lindy brought her husband Dave and daughter Robyn to visit us in Northern Ireland (a good excuse for us all to 'do' Belfast and the Titanic exhibition together). We went on a cruise to the Canaries over Christmas and New Year 2012/13 on the Marco Polo. We both enjoyed it, though we had a few problems on board as Paul had some difficulty in finding his way around the ship, and especially in finding a toilet at increasingly frequent intervals. Fortunately the steward was very helpful. Later that year, we went to Canada to see Paul's other daughter, Karen, in Mississauga, and to Prague to stay with Niall, Bara and my brand new grandson Toby. And there were weekend outings to Londonderry, the Giant's Causeway and the Bushmills distillery, and a train trip to visit friends in Galway.

Meanwhile, the Alzheimer's diagnosis was indeed confirmed. It came to take over more and more of Paul's life, and coping with it came to take over more of mine. Signs of dementia became evident in his driving. Sometimes he got lost, and on one occasion found himself miles away in another town. He became more dependent on

167

me thinking ahead regarding his needs, and tended to get into difficult situations when I was not with him.

A sample of diary entries for 2012–13 reminds me how I could take less and less for granted:

Thursday 22nd November 2012

I was tired and decided to go to bed early (about nine). Had a nice bath, and settled down with a book. Paul had been out in the workshop after tea and I asked him to check the lights and heater were off, also the house lights and TV. This he seemed to do and he said were all done, so we drifted off. I woke later (not sure when but maybe around midnight), worried that although he had said the garage heater and lights were all off, he might have just done the lights. So I put on slippers and dressing gown, got a torch, and went outside. Lights were off, but both electric heaters were on full blast! Not much point in saying anything to him about it, but made mental note to always check for myself, even when it means going outside late at night when I'm tired or already gone to bed.

Saturday 24th November 2012

Last winter we had a problem to do with lighting the open fire in the lounge. It's a Baxi with an ash tin that needs to be emptied when full. Paul put the whole tin plus ash into the bin and proceeded to light the fire as usual. The problem was only discovered when the grate needed to be emptied again, and there was no tin! It had gone to the waste disposal dump. We had to empty the grate basin manually and suck out the last bit of ash with a wet-and-dry vacuum, then buy a new tin on eBay. After that I watched to make sure it was emptied and replaced each time. Today it was emptied and brought back in a plastic binbag. The fire was duly lit, but went out as Paul forgot to put any coal on it. I offered to relight it, but discovered that the tin was still in the bag on the floor! So the vacuum was brought out again to suck out the small amount of ash in the pit.

Sunday 2nd December 2012

Another load of washing... the machine and I never seem to stop work! The weather has now turned cold and I do sympathise, but Paul's continual obsession with shutting doors (in a centrally heated bungalow) is driving me crazy! He sits for hours reading the paper; no wonder he gets cold. While I busy myself washing towels, filling the washing machine and dishwasher, emptying them, making meals, setting the table, clearing the table… and all I get as I go in and out of the kitchen is 'Shut the door, darling!' I show him the thermometer, which shows equal temperatures in all rooms, and he says it means nothing.

Tuesday 12th February 2013

There have been several episodes recently:

> 1.Paul took the car to buy some coal just before I needed to go out for a girls' night, and didn't return. He got lost and the police spotted the car on the M1 near Lurgan. No mobile phone with him.

2. *While I was at the dentist, Paul went into the glen behind the house to get a tarpaulin that had blown away, and he didn't come back. He had no mobile phone with him again. The police were informed, and helicopters and next door's dog found him in the glen unable to move.*

3. *I work at the Oxfam shop 11am-2pm on Fridays. He goes out for coffee/lunch, but comes into the shop before I finish, demanding I go back home.*

There were moments when battle lines were drawn. We bought some Ikea furniture for the bungalow: a sofa delivered ready-made, and a recliner chair which had to be assembled. A skilled woodworker, Paul was keen to do this husbandly job, so I left him to it, or at least I tried to. I noticed he had tipped out the parts on the rug, with what looked like a million screws, washers and nuts. I could see the parts were not being counted and checked against the instruction leaflet, so I offered to do that for him. He bristled and refused the offer. I suggested instead that I could count the small screws to make sure they were all there, but that annoyed him too, as he had always worked with his hands and making bespoke furniture had been part of his business. Now I was beginning to worry, and tried to gently put the screws, washers and nuts into small piles.

"No!" he shouted, "I'll do it!" He physically pushed me away.

"But that's the way you have to do Ikea furniture; it's not like the things you used to make from scratch," I argued. Without thinking, I took his arm to steer him away.

"No!" he shouted, this time loudly, and pushed me backwards.

"But I'm trying to help you!"

"I don't need your help! Give me that piece!" His eyes flashed, but I knew I was right and had to take over. The push became a shove, delivered with more energy and even anger. We had got into a real fight before we knew what was happening. I could see how angry he was, and the push had hurt my arm as well as my feelings. I struck back. And then I remembered what we had been talking about at the Alzheimer's café: 'Divert, Distract, Deflect.' And, stepping back, I decided that this was not the way to go!

I learned to look for activities we could share on a more equal footing, like church and travel. Paul helped redecorate our new bungalow home in Holywood, Co Down; became involved in the local community: church, coffee shops and Men's Shed; and took courses in pottery in nearby Newtownards. We loved going for walks by the shore and Scrabo Tower.

In the summer of 2013 we took off for the south of England to visit Paul's friends and relatives in Hampshire and my daughter in London. The trip turned out to be rather eventful. The flight to Southampton was via Edinburgh, where we had to go through security again and nearly got in trouble for the perfume bottle found in Paul's backpack. Fortunately it was under 100ml. Hiring a car at Southampton, we drove to Stockbridge, where Paul had lived before coming to join me in Ireland. We walked, very slowly, along the streets he used to know. He recognised his cousin's house, where he had lived for a while, but didn't want to visit his own flat. We visited his friend Sandy, but the journey proved more complicated than it should have been, because Paul didn't tell me in time about turning off to the right.

Next day we went to see Paul's granddaughter and new great-granddaughter at Petersfield, before spending an interesting few hours doing the shops and cathedral in Winchester, which he knew well. Then we set off for his cousin Olive's house. All went well until we got to the roundabout. 'This way!' 'You sure?' 'Yes!' But no, we were lost – twice! The local paper boy rescued us; we got there, and the evening went very well.

On our last full day, we drove to Jenny's new home in London. Being Sunday, the M3 was quiet, but we found the house chaotic as they had just moved in. Paul enjoyed the children and the chat. But by next morning he had had enough and wanted to leave. And I found I had a parking ticket – my own fault for parking half on the pavement and expecting our Blue Badge for disabled parking to cover us for all eventualities, but I'd have appreciated some moral support from my husband! We left earlier than really necessary and had a good drive down to Southampton – until I was directed to the station car park instead of the airport. Then it was the wrong car park at the airport, and by the time we found the car-hire office Paul needed a toilet so I was left to carry all the bags! At check-in we had, 'Why are we checking in? Where are we going?' Home, I explained. 'But we are at home' – meaning his old home in Hampshire. He couldn't understand the long wait for our plane and tried to get me to queue up for other planes instead. And just before our flight boarded, there was another urgent toilet call. But we did get on our way at last, and were glad to get home.

By September 2013, things had definitely moved on, but there were still highs and lows. As I wrote in my diary:

So yesterday (Saturday) he didn't like my 'attitude'. Well, I was annoyed because he had lost not just his house and car keys, but also the back door key he used to replace them. The previous day was Friday and as usual I was doing my stint from 11 to two at Oxfam. It was a lovely sunny morning and I suggested he walk down to town about lunch time and find me at the shop. We were going to have lunch at Café Nero, pay the final amount to the travel agent for our Canada trip, and see the doctor at four. No sign of him at one, so I phoned the house and his mobile, several times, but had no reply from either. I did a few messages, and drove up to the house. He was not there, but the front door was locked and a neighbour said he saw him heading down to town with a floppy hat on his head. Back to town, but no sign of him. I had a coffee at Café Nero and they said they'd look out for him, so I drove back home using the other route: he was not there. I drove down that way again, looking out for him, but still no sign or any response from his phone. I had another coffee, and at last he appeared, hatless, but with the hat in his hand.

So the story was, he had set off but as he was near the doctor's surgery had popped in to use the toilet on the way, so was late coming down to meet me at the café. And the keys? He had mislaid his bunch a few days previously, and so had decided to take the back door key, locking the front door (but NOT the back one!) Now the back door key was missing too. We had a search and decided to look tomorrow as we had a message that my mobile phone had been returned from repair, so we set off to the ee shop (twice, as I forgot the lead for the phone they had loaned me), had a meal on the way back and relaxed the rest of the evening.

On Saturday we started looking again for the keys, and by lunchtime found them in the glove box of the car; not before I had sounded off a bit about the cost of replacing them. Consequently the atmosphere in the house was icy, although outside was warm and

173

sunny. But finding that bunch of keys improved things, and we went on to get the BBQ out and had a lovely evening in the garden, listening to music on the iPod and the new tiny loudspeaker he had got me for Christmas. With our mood improving, we went to bed and had the nicest cuddle. And so it goes…

The last holiday we had before Alzheimer's prevented us from using airports was a cruise to Norway and the Shetlands to see the most spectacular country I have ever been to.

With Alzheimer's, there can be problems on board a ship, such as being convinced the cabin door you try to open with your pass card is indeed your cabin. It looks just like it, though the number is not quite the same. And fortunately, this meant it would not open the door! At the meal table, the waiter helpfully showed us the wine list. I hesitated, wondering if this was the list of wines not included in the all-inclusive… so as I hesitated, he topped up my wine from the previous night's bottle, and Paul's too, and before long we were well tiddly! Not so good going to bed when I had to make sure his bed stayed dry. But overall the trip was a success.

Being on board a cruise ship is great, as there is little chance of losing your husband. Or at least, you know they must be somewhere on the ship! But day trips can be a hazard, so I had to be really alert at all times, especially when getting on and off coaches. One man who was suspected of having Alzheimer's (but was actually just a bit deaf) got on the wrong coach and ended up in the wrong town, but managed to get a train and then a taxi back to the ship. So Paul and I stayed hand in hand most of the time.

On one trip I sat down beside a lady who was travelling alone. We had exchanged a few words on the small boat taking us ashore, and she had really taken to Paul. On the coach he had decided to sit on the very front seat of the coach near the driver. So I took the seat behind, and chatted with this lady, asking, as you do, 'And what do you do?' 'I'm a writer,' she replied. 'Oh, what do you write about?' I asked. 'Crime novels!!' 'Wow', I thought, great choice of seat! And it turned out she had about 30 novels on Amazon, and not only that – although she sounded English, she lived in Kircubbin. With the cruise leaving from Belfast, it was mostly Irish and Northern Irish passengers. So we chatted about books and the sort of books we read, and book clubs we had joined. I talked about belonging to a book club called Bookcrossing. com, which has made an impact on my reading over the last few years. I'm a keen though not very fast reader, and Bookcrossing has actually changed my reading habits. As a child I had practically lived in the library, which was then situated in my school, Rosetta Primary, until it moved to a brand new building near the Ormeau Bridge. For me the two-mile walk was nothing, just to get another book. Later, when I had children, I didn't read as much, as there were too many distractions, so Bookcrossing arrived just when I needed it. And it gave me a new way to give karma in the form of sharing with total strangers wonderful books I had read and enjoyed. As well as really helping me start to organise my books and my reading, Bookcrossing helped me find a new way to carry out 'random acts of kindness'. I released one of my first books at the airport, and someone immediately 'caught it' as we say, and wrote on the website page for the book: 'It made my day!'

So in Norway I shared with my new friend the book I had just finished reading, and we agreed to meet after we came home. Free plug here for the author – her name is Jo Bannister! She brought me a copy of one of her books, the third in a series, called The Depths of Solitude, a Brodie Farrell mystery, and (to cut this story short) I loved it, and went on to read more in the series.

Back at home, the Alzheimer's Society became a great resource for help and advice. At one point, at an Alzheimer's party, Paul sought out the staff worker who had helped us from the beginning, and asked her straight out, 'What is the future for me, how will Alzheimer's affect me?' She told him honestly, 'There is no cure.' He accepted this, and came to accept my help more willingly as his condition deteriorated. He would say, 'Bossy Boots!' with a twinkle in his eye, when I suggested options.

At last the Alzheimer's won. Paul could not be left alone, and the arthritis in my knees made it difficult for me to manage his physical needs. We started having a regular care worker slot on Fridays so I could carry on helping out at the Oxfam shop, then on other days so I could go to hospital appointments, then every morning to get Paul up, washed and dressed, then three times a day. Although he still recognised me, he had no idea where he was, or what day it was, and had difficulty finding his way around the house. It came to the point where the social worker advised me to consider a residential home for Paul, where he could have constant supervision.

The first care home that we found for Paul was quite far away, 27 miles in fact. It was situated right on the coast at the end of the Ards peninsula, about a mile beyond the little seaside town of Portaferry. Since his diagnosis of Alzheimer's, about three years ago, we had been getting to know this peninsula, and Paul had come to love it. He had been going once a week to a pottery class at Ards Arts Centre and twice to a day centre in Newtownards. During my first marriage, Chris and I had lived for a time in Killinchy on the other side of Strangford Lough, and he had developed his business around the area of Newtownards at the head of the lough. So I had got to know the little towns around the lough: Comber, Killinchy, Newtownards, Kircubbin and Portaferry. And just after Paul's diagnosis, the Alzheimer's Society directed us to the newly formed Memory Café, which met in Comber. So Wednesday mornings usually found us driving over the Holywood hills through

Craigantlet, turning right at that awful staggered crossroads, through Dundonald (where Chris and I had our first house) and on down the winding country road to Comber. There we got to know other couples and singles coping with this same dreadful disease, and formed good friendships.

Two days after Christmas 2014, Paul went into care. I wrote: 'On this day (27/12/2014) I physically gave up the battle of the last few years: the wet beds, the airport hassles, the long car journey preparations, the short car journey preparations, the loss of logical discussions; against the cuddles, the company, the compliments and the sheer presence of him in the house with me. I finished packing up his essentials, put them in the car, helped him on with his coat, and drove the 30 miles to the end of the peninsula that is called Ards, to the beautiful little town of Portaferry.'

Paul settled in very well, unlike many residents who were constantly asking to go home. He had a lovely room overlooking the sea, with the Mourne Mountains in the distance, and he informed me his own boat was tied up just out of sight, ready for us to take a trip when we wished to. Although it was a fairly long journey, and the road was narrow and twisty, the scenery was beautiful and I did enjoy the drive. Until winter came, and huge waves often came lashing across the windscreen.

Portaferry was just a bit further along the road from Kircubbin, where Jo Bannister lived. So I broke my journey on some occasions to share tea and scones with my new-found writer friend. And Jo got to know us both, to the extent that Paul often asked for her, though for some strange Alzheimer's-related reason, he always called her Anne.

Paul was very content at Portaferry; in fact we had our last 'weekend away' there, when I took him to the local hotel for a treat.

He dressed in his nice gold evening jacket, we had a three-course meal with wine, and shared a bed for the last time together.

Because it was such a long drive to Portaferry, I kept looking for alternative residential places nearer to Holywood for Paul. He had used various care homes for respite when I went to visit family, so we had a fair idea of the good ones and the frankly bad. One of these he refused to go back to, and another we rejected because of poor staffing levels, care and cleanliness. Eventually we were offered a 'Fold' room in Holywood, which was designed for people with early Alzheimer's and was only a few minutes' drive from home. After some months, however, Paul was becoming uncooperative and difficult to take out in the car, and it became too time-consuming for the staff to deal with his showering, dressing and other increasing needs.

At that point he moved into a large home in Bangor, only 15 minutes' drive from our home, with a separate section for advanced dementia patients. Paul settled in well and still greeted me every day with, 'Lovely to see you.' From there we could Skype or Facetime with his family in the USA and Canada. Lindy, Karen and his son Stephen in Australia also came to visit from time to time. He still enjoyed reading magazines or books with pictures, and listening to music on headphones or the speaker from my iPod. One of the first CDs we used to enjoy together when we first met was by Jake Thackray – we found we each had a copy – and I brought it to play in his room. Colds and chest infections tended to affect him badly. The care was excellent, but gradually he became less mobile and his speech and swallowing deteriorated.

I realised Paul would not remember things I told him. However, he still seemed to enjoy reading in small bursts, so I wrote him a letter that he could read as often as he wanted. It would probably feel like the first time every time he read it.

Dearest Paul

It has been a hard time for us both. You know you were diagnosed with Alzheimer's Disease five years ago. At first it did not affect us much, but soon I was not able to care for you, so I found you a care home in Holywood where you would be well cared for.

But then it got worse, and the Holywood care home could not care for you either. So I found you a nursing home in Bangor where they are equipped to care for people with Alzheimer's, and that is where you are now. I hope you will get to know the carers there, they are very good. And I will come to see you every   week.

It may not be what you really want your life to be, but sadly with Alzheimer's this is the only choice. You are now nearly 80 years old, you have done very well. I love you so much and wish it could be otherwise. Please be happy and accept things as they are here.

All my love, my darling, I will be there for you when you need me, as you were for me when I needed you.

Norah

So in the care home Paul regained his comfort, dignity and contentment. But the ability to read even a verse of a poem gradually left him. He could not catch my eye in recognition when I arrived, the birthday cake seemed irrelevant, and even swallowing a mouthful of coffee became impossible.

In mid-January 2018 he got a chest infection. In hospital it became aspiration pneumonia due to his inability to swallow, with food going to his lungs and causing infection. A week in hospital on antibiotics helped, but doctors advised that another course would only prolong the problem. His concerned family joined me at his bedside, sad for his inability to show his recognition except by movement of a toe under the bedclothes. With his doctors, we decided together to take him back to his room in care and keep him warm and comfortable. After three days, on 23rd January, he passed away peacefully in his sleep, having lived a long and full life, loved and cared for by good people and knowing he was adored by his family and myself.

His daughters and family stayed on for the funeral, and we all participated in saying goodbye to a beloved father, grandfather and husband. On a sunny day some weeks later, Jo Bannister and I scattered his ashes on Strangford Lough, a place he knew well and loved, and a part of the sea that had always been in his life.

Requiem, Paul, may your soul rest in peace.

Here is a poem I wrote for Paul in 2016:

> *Slipping away from me, I prematurely mourn his loss*
> *He is still there, and looking just the same.*
> *But stubbornness and nonsense take control.*
> *'Lovely to see you' losing all its meaning*
> *As that is where it ends.*
> *With basic self-attention, independence gone, what else is left?*
> *The love of music drifting in and out as CD turns.*
>
> *A nudge in church, and fingers underline some tender words.*
> *I do respond, loving the words he briefly underlines,*
> *Then face the journey home, resistance to comply.*

A love once all-consuming, now just a memory sweet.
Our joy in music, books and travels shared in eight short
years.

How   cruel   is   this   human   suffering,
Affecting more the loved than he who loves.

On the steps of my Holywood apartment

Exploring his new surroundings, together in Belfast

*Welcoming Paul to Northern Ireland, at the Ulster Transport
Museum. He loved his cars!*

Our wedding at Old St Peters Church, Stockbridge, Hampshire

The 30 guests at our wedding in Stockbridge

The little seaside town of Portaferry, where Paul's ashes were scattered

7

EXPLORING MY FAMILY TREE

In 1998 I began putting together our family tree, both my branch and Chris's. As I wrote in my Christmas letter that year, it was 'an exciting and fulfilling task, which has meant getting to know many of the older and less well-known (to me) members of the various branches of the Brown and Anderson families. The Anderson branch has been exciting because with the help of Uncle Joe's book, Anderson of Flush and Bawn I have been able to enter names and dates back to 1543'. It was also interesting to make contact with the families of my father-in-law Harry Brown's four brothers Arthur, Herbert, Bob and John (Jack), most of whom I never knew existed. Jack named his son Harry and followed him to Australia. I met Bob's daughter Myrtle; Arthur's son Fred; and Herbert's widow Florence and one of her daughters and grandchildren. I also had several letters from Fred's mother Mabel in Rhode Island. She had an interesting story to tell, as recounted in the 'Arthur and Mabel Brown' section below. More recently, I have made the acquaintance of – and in 2016 visited – McCoubrey family members in New York, relatives on my mother's side who I never knew. And there were more Wilson relatives, one of them local and one American, and an Australian who was related through the Andersons from Sixmilecross in Tyrone and came to visit me in 2018. I have also made contact with uncles and cousins in England, Northern Ireland, Australia and the USA.

I started taking an interest in my family tree after my uncle Joseph Anderson, my father's eldest brother, showed me a family tree he had drawn up, which he had framed and displayed in his home. He would tell us how he had researched the details using as his main source a publication written by his ancestor Robert Hall Anderson in 1900, and how he had later travelled to America to meet some of his connected relatives. He also showed us a document called 'Letters Patent', which seemed very complicated to me as a child, but I kept it in the back of my mind. Years later, I discovered how the software Family Tree Maker made it easy to draw up a family tree and save it online. Buying the software was a quite random purchase, done with no research whatsoever, but it sparked my interest and I started adding names on my computer, remembering what my uncle had told me. I found that he had written a revised edition of Robert Hall Anderson's publication, which contained a large amount of information going back as far as 1543 in Scotland. As Uncle Joseph wrote, 'Many such northern Ireland families could until last century trace back to first settlement here in the XVII and XVIII centuries. Now with loss of records from the activities of modern housewives, new farm construction, changes in land tenure, and general loss of interest in family records, their line of descent from a Scottish, English or Welsh settler or a native Irish clansman is in most cases lost.'

Using my computer, I continued constructing my own family tree. I had great satisfaction copying the records of births, marriages and deaths from my uncle's book and following these up by visiting relatives to get their stories to add to the details. As people married and had children, these names were then added.

For a time, life became busy for me as I had started a new job. Much later, I thought I must get back to this tree and see if I could still add details. The software basics were still on my computer, but sadly out of date. I researched how to get another copy of the software, with no success, but eventually discovered that it had been taken over by ancestry.com, and I was able to link my software to this site. This was a great move forward. I bought an up-to-date copy of the Family Tree Maker software, and started adding details again to my tree, which by then had nearly 1,000 entries. I was suddenly full of a great zeal to update it for the sake of my children and those who would follow.

My mother was a great source of information until she died in 1999. One of the interesting things about my tree was that my mother, Muriel, and father, Catherwood Anderson, were related, though not by blood, as I explained in Chapter 1. My mother's own mother, Norah Wilson, had died when Muriel was 12, and her father remarried. Her stepmother, Ethel, had several sisters, one of whom had five children. Muriel was introduced to this family, and one of the sons, Catherwood Anderson, was to become my father.

A difficulty I had in trying to research my family tree, and I don't know if my uncle found this a problem too, was that both my mother's family and my father's family at some stage converted from the mainstream Presbyterian church into the small denomination called the Brethren. The Brethren conducted some burials in Presbyterian churchyards, but had no church records of their baptisms. This was because the Brethren baptised their members as adults, and as far as I know did not keep records of these. Another relevant point is that war records have been of little use, because few of my non-conformist ancestors became soldiers. So, following the burning of the Public Record Office in Dublin in 1922, it was hard to find any records, and my uncle Joe was dependent on 'such other sources in both Ireland and Scotland as are extant and known' to him. These will have included other church records, and I am very grateful to him for searching them. Nowadays there are also many websites that can be used to find data.

Back to Robert Hall Anderson. For his 1900 first edition of *Anderson of Flush and Bawn* he drew on both written and oral sources. He was born in 1848, and says that as a boy and young man he 'listened and carefully treasured the oft-told story of his forebears and their doings, which went back to the reign of Mary Queen of Scots'. He also had resource to 'the family muniments, local estate papers, his grand-uncle's manuscripts and private family records in Scotland'. His uncle, the Reverend Archibald Armstrong of Dervaghroy, Presbytery of Omagh, 'left considerable information relative to the Armstrong, Hall and Anderson history.... In 1874 (he) visited Greenock, Paisley, Aberdeen, Bridge of Weir, Perth, Edinburgh and Dumfries in Scotland', and 'the report of his investigation was given in a letter to J.M. Anderson of Minnesota, Minneapolis in 1900, which was used to write this book.'

So, on with the story. In 1575 Joseph Anderson, a merchant of Paisley, had a son, Archibald, who enlisted as one of the Scottish yeomen under Sir Paul Gore for service in Northern Ireland. He landed at Donaghadee in 1602 with his three grandsons, Simon, Patrick and Archibald Armstrong. Interesting stories taken from my uncle's book include 'the family record of the marriage of Donald Armstrong, Alexander's son, to Margaret Anderson, Joseph's daughter of Paisley, at Bridge of Weir in the middle of the 16th century, with John Knox officiating. Three sons of that union were also in Goare's forces landing at Donaghadee in Ireland in 1602.' Another fascinating story from that time is of 'the only Scottish martyr of the name, William Anderson, a burger of Perth. He, his wife, Hellen Stirke, and three others were tried on the morrow after

St Paul's day (1543 old reckoning, 1544 new reckoning), and put to death there on a charge that the men imported the scriptures in the common tongue and held and taught the reformed faith, and that the woman had dishonoured Mary the mother of our Lord by praying directly to God while in child bed. And it was thus that the young Archibald Anderson came to Ulster in the North of Ireland and later to settle there, and to found at Flush and Bawn, adjoining Sixmilecross in the county of Tyrone, the now widespread family of Anderson, the descendants of this history.'

My uncle then went on to describe in Chapter V, 'The Great Plantation of Ulster in 1608-1620', 'the systems of farming, and how the demesne lands were for the owners' use, as distinct from those which under Plantation terms he was required to settle with tenants.'

Researching my family tree took me in all sorts of directions. Finding out about the people I knew well and those who were close to them was the easy bit. Most families know a little bit about other families to whom they are related, but who distance themselves in a way that says, 'This far and no further...' It could be shyness, or a feeling that they are higher up or lower down the social scale. They may not even know why. I was told that my mother had an 'inferiority complex', which apparently meant that she felt she was not as accomplished as those in her social circle. This made no sense to me. Perhaps it was because her mother died when she was 12, and a stepmother took charge who had no children of her own. I'll never know why, but one thing I did know – I did not want to be like that! Yes, I was quite shy at first, but as I left home and developed as an adult, I had no fear of talking to people as equals. To me it seemed just as wrong to look down on people as to envy them. Everyone had something good to offer; you just needed to talk to them about it. And maybe that was why I got nicknamed 'Nosy Norah'!

Here are some of the people I came across in my research.

Elsie and Muriel

I first met my mother's cousin Elsie Jones in September 1989 on her visit to Ireland. She was 78 and had lived mainly in England; I later discovered she had spent some of her childhood in Twickenham, just across the road from the house my daughter and her husband bought in 2013.

Elsie wrote me many letters between 1992 and 2001. She was an excellent typist and would use odd scraps of paper, often the back of a picture she liked, and when she ran out of space she adjusted the typewriter to print along the edge or the top of the page. She also sent out long Christmas circulars to her many friends and relations, 180 of them she said, detailing her activities throughout the past year.

Elsie was born on 25th June 1911 at Woodford, Essex, the eldest daughter of my mother's aunt Florrie. According to Elsie, she was named after her father's first sweetheart. She was a committed Christian and attended a Congregational church, so I think in a lot of ways she and I were quite similar in our beliefs and practices. The first milestone in her journey to faith came at the age of ten when she 'met Jesus' in a vivid dream following a series of children's addresses at the Twickenham United Reformed Church she attended. The first address was 'How to tell a real lady', which probably influenced how she would conduct the rest of her life. The second address, 'Florence Nightingale', also represented the second milestone, as it determined her choice of career. In the dream, she saw a large table with children walking round it, and Jesus walking with them with his arm round each of them in turn. He told her 'You are to be a missionary nurse in India,' and from then on she never had any other ambition. She was accepted for nurse training at the Middlesex Hospital at age 17, and bought a second-hand uniform in anticipation of beginning missionary work at age 21. But one day she had an accident on the hockey field while playing for her old school team. She damaged her spine, and it ended forever her plan to be a nurse. Elsie's plans were shattered. She applied nonetheless to the London Missionary Society Home Staff in Westminster, which seemed to her the next best way to follow her dream, and argued her way into a job there.

The third milestone was meeting Muriel Fairhill at Livingstone House, 'the most wonderful character I ever met'. After Muriel's father died in 1946, she and Elsie set up home together at Tunbridge Wells. It only occurred to me on re-reading her letters after her death that she was possibly gay.

Elsie often spoke with admiration about Father Elias Chacour, Archbishop of the Melkite Catholic Church of Akko, Haifa, Nazareth and all Galilee and author of the book, Blood Brothers. Elsie supported the Muslim cause in the Palestine issue, believing the Palestinians had the right to recover their land from the Israelis. She would argue fiercely with my mother, who backed the Jews. Also, my mother felt doctrine was the most important consideration, but for Elsie it was love. Years later I read an article in our church magazine of October 2015 saying exactly that; it was after I had left the regular Presbyterian Church in Ireland and joined the Non-Subscribing Presbyterian Church of Ireland, which was linked to Elsie's church.

Elsie was the oldest and longest surviving of three sisters. She was fiercely independent but had a very soft heart. She never married, saying her only sweetheart had died at a young age of lung cancer. Her sister Winnie was unable to have children, but she and her husband adopted one daughter, and Elsie was very fond of this niece. Her other sister Dorothy (Dorrie, the 'scamp' who my mother said had come with Aunt Florrie to look after her when her mother, my

193

Grandmother Norah, died in 1932) joined the ATS in 1939, was promoted to Corporal, received a special commendation from the Red Cross, and then joined the Civil Service. While serving in the ATS, she fell in love with a married officer called Teddy and went to live with him – an unforgiveable sin according to my mother. Teddy eventually divorced his first wife, but in my mother's eyes Dorrie never repented of her 'sin'. Later she and her husband ran a delicatessen business in Southsea.

Elsie's parents died tragically in Amsterdam in 1953 when, forgetting the Dutch drove on the right, they stepped off a tram into oncoming traffic. Elsie herself lived to age 94. She spent her later years at Lomas House in Worthing, a retirement home run by the London Missionary Society but taken over in 2001 by the United Reformed Church Southern Province Synod. By then the home had only six residents, who were aged between 70 and 99, and was earmarked for future use as a conference centre. When I visited Elsie there in 2001 with my cousin Lynn, she had just been registered as partially sighted. A new lens in one eye helped her type, but reading had become too difficult and she declared she was grateful to 'whoever invented television'. Nonetheless, she took us to see a church at Goring-by-Sea, the English Martyrs Catholic Church, which had a ceiling painted in the style of the Sistine Chapel. Elsie took a genuine interest in my children and also in the men in my life. She died on 12th June 2005, but I felt she would have been delighted when I married Paul, who was an Englishman, five years later.

Fred Godden

In 2006, I had a letter from a solicitor in Dublin named Julian Deale, asking me if I was related to a Fred Godden who lived in Dublin. Yes, I said, he was my mother's first cousin. I had visited him a few years back and he had kept in touch regularly, usually around Christmas, but I had not heard from him for a few years.

It turned out that, as I had suspected, Fred Godden had died. He had been living on his own and had few relatives, namely his nephew Paul and niece Bernadette, who were his brother Gabriel's twins and, as far as I knew, lived in Dublin, and his cousin Elsie Jones, who lived in England. He himself had been married, but had no children of his own. I remember him as a very sweet old man, and other members of the family spoke of him with great affection. His wife Charlotte had died 20 years previously, and his cousin Elsie was not married, so the two of them had always kept in touch until she died in 2005.

It was after my own mother had died in 1999 that I decided to make contact with Fred and go and see him at his home in Dublin. He welcomed me into his modest abode, and chatted about his relatives and his interests, reminiscing about my mother and her family. He suggested we go out for a meal in the nearby Clontarf Castle, which was now a very nice modern hotel. I had never been there before and was very impressed with his choice. He was a delightful companion, and had dressed himself up in his best clothes for the occasion. I had no idea how well off he might be, but in the true style of a gentleman he insisted on paying for the meal, which was by no means cheap.

Subsequently, Fred continued to send me a Christmas card every year until the year he died. I was sad when the cards stopped coming but could not find out more as I had no contact details for any of his relatives in Dublin. So it was not really a surprise when Mr Deale phoned me. I was asked to go and see him in Dublin, and I remember taking the train to Connolly Station, and then the DART to his office on Monkstown Road, South Dublin. It was a beautiful sunny day, and I enjoyed the short walk from the train station to his office.

It appeared Fred had been renting the house where he was living, and he had left some money but no will. Mr Deale asked if I knew where Fred's nephew and niece lived, which sadly I didn't. There had been hushed talk of the nephew Paul's marriage to an Italian Catholic (his sister Bernadette's husband's sister apparently), and that was all I knew. As Protestants living in Catholic Ireland, Paul's family had not approved of the match. I said I would try and find out what I could, but with Elsie now dead, there were no other relatives who might know.

I found Mr Deale a fascinating person. We chatted for quite some time, and he gave me a copy of a book he wrote – about Dublin murders, I think. In the end I asked if I could go and see Fred's house while I was so close, and he contacted the woman who owned the house for permission to make entry. I said I was not interested in any of his belongings, except perhaps any family photos, or his books, of which I had noticed on my previous visit he had many. A time was arranged, and I drove to the house on 55 Howth Road in Clontarf, Dublin 3. I knocked on the door but no one came to open it. I waited around for an hour or two and contacted Mr Deale to say I could not gain access, but he was not able to contact the landlady. I suspected she thought I was after something, and she never turned up. I wandered around the outside of the house, looking for anything I could take as a memento of this lovely uncle. The garden was overgrown and the house in poor repair. All I could find was a little brass ash tray in the shape of a clam shell, which I still have. Unfortunately, Mr Deale must have found the niece and nephew, as I never heard from him again!

Uncle Arthur Anderson

In 2016 my uncle Arthur died at the family farm in Aghalee, which he had been running for 80 years. My brother (also called Arthur) and I had many happy memories of childhood holidays on the farm, where Uncle Arthur, his sister Aunt Doreen and his wife Joyce welcomed us whenever we turned up and where they looked after us during the times when our mother was ill. Arthur and Joyce had three children: William, Kathryn and Sylvia.

This is the address, minimally abridged, which my brother gave at Uncle Arthur's funeral. His words reflect Arthur's personality, his faith and the depth of our love and respect for him.

It is a privilege for me to pay tribute to my Uncle Arthur. As a very young lad, when my mother was ill, Arthur and Joyce took me into their home for summer months. He was a second dad to me during those formative days, teaching me about chickens, pigs and cows, teaching me how to drive on his "wee grey Fergie" and in his Reliant three-wheeler van. I so enjoyed those wonderful days, not least Auntie Joyce's sponge cake, which has never been bettered in my experience!

As we remember Arthur's life, I want us to consider how he, as should we all, lived it in the light of the example set by our Lord Jesus Christ.

William Arthur Anderson and his twin brother David Oliver were born on September 14th 1924, in Stewartstown, Tyrone, Northern Ireland, the youngest of their family. Sadly, David Oliver died in infancy, but Arthur lived to be the oldest living of his family. To my sister Norah and to myself, he always seemed great fun and more exciting than some other members of our wider family! He was always interested in the family, and in the family tree his brother Joseph had researched and which Norah now continues to develop online.

Arthur's father William was 58 and their mother Edith was 42 when he was born. But in 1927, when Uncle Arthur was just a lad, his dad had a stroke, which left him unable to speak ever again. He died on 6th June 1934 and his mother had to sell the family farm in Maguires Bridge and move to Ulsterville Ave in Belfast. Then on 1st February 1936, they moved from there to the Methodist Manse at Craigmore – just across the road from here. And shortly after, on the 24th February 1936, they hatched their first 123 chickens. So Uncle Arthur farmed on this site for 80 years, looking after animals and short shelf-life products; work which could have left little time for the other things which matter in life. Even when his mobility was weakening over the last few weeks, he could be found spending time around the farm on his electric scooter or being driven around by his grand-daughter Sarah in her field car.

On 18th September 1957, Arthur married a beautiful young lady from Wicklow called Joyce Robb. My sister Norah was a bridesmaid when she was just 11, and she remembers the thrill of wearing her first grown-up formal dress. I can vividly remember meeting Auntie Joyce for the first time in the front lounge of the manse across the road. Joyce and Arthur were not ostentatious, but friendly and kind and good people. They were generous and hospitable to many and supported the work of missionaries overseas and evangelists at home.

I asked his family what they will most remember about their dad.

"He was always there. His steadfastness, determination, perseverance. Of a practical nature, and always keen to help others learn by giving them his full instructions. Always willing to help. Kind. Always interested in the family. Encylopaedia Britannica, geography, sightseeing. Family devotions around the scriptures, particularly the Psalms. Never stern or narrow minded. Private, thoughtful and reflective."

The Catherwoods

My father's mother, Grandmother Anderson, was a Catherwood by birth. The Catherwoods came across to me as a wealthy branch of the family, but it later became apparent that there were two types of Catherwoods: the more religious ones who read and even wrote theological books, and the more secular (and more financially wealthy ones), who had large houses and owned race horses. We only ever heard stories about them!

When I joined a large Presbyterian church, which had a reputation of being a 'socially climbing' church, I soon found out that a Catherwood called Harry was a member there, with his second wife, who had presented a children's TV programme. My mother disapproved of second marriages, especially when the first wife was still alive, so feelings towards most of the Catherwoods were frosty, and the gap between the two types widened. On the other hand, the more religious Catherwoods were completely accepted, and even looked up to.

Anyway, the time came when Harry died and it was announced from the pulpit that all were welcome to the house after the funeral. I decided to go in the interests of family history and developing the family tree. It was a large house in a well-to-do area, and the welcome was warm. Glass of wine in hand, I chatted with Harry's youngest daughter Andrea, an ITV presenter, and then unfortunately in the crowd I knocked over a large vase of flowers in the hall, and the vase shattered. The hostess was polite but cold, and she now seems not to recognise me when we meet in the street.

Another Catherwood, Fred, who married the daughter of a famous London preacher, John Stott, was much admired by my family but still kept a certain distance. His father, Stewart, my grandmother's brother, owned the Rosapenna Hotel in Donegal, where my mother's sister Myra was manageress for a time. Great-uncle Stewart was an enigma: a social climber who espoused the evangelical Christian tradition and often invited preachers to stay.

And it was only after my mother-in-law Lilla Brown died that I discovered letters written from Rosapenna by her husband Harry, my father-in-law, when he attended a Christian conference and had a room in the hotel – an early and unwitting link between my family and the Browns. I was amazed to read that Harry felt quite insulted to be given a room that was nothing more than a boxroom, and demanded to be moved to something larger. And his personal impression of the hotel owner was nothing if not cynical regarding his Christian witness!

Here is the letter Harry wrote to Lilla from Rosapenna:

Sunday

Hullo darling

200

Have just had breakfast and as I have nothing to do until 4 p.m. I thought I would spend some of the time writing you a few lines and incidentally using a few sheets of Catherwood's nice notepaper!

I just got to town yesterday in the nick of time to get the train to Strabane. It was crowded and I had to buy a 1st class in order to get on at all. Had a good sleep in a very comfortable first class seat. In fact I slept all the way from Belfast to Dungannon. It was worth travelling 1st class to get that good sleep. From Dungannon to Strabane I had the company of a good-looking ATS officer. She knew the Far East well from books and was keen to listen about China.

At Strabane I was met by Catherwood's man and his station wagon. I have seldom enjoyed anything as much as the 47½ miles from Strabane to Rosapenna. The country is exquisite and we were travelling yesterday just as the sun was dipping behind the hills and the shadows played all kinds of marvellous tricks as they ran up and down the hills. Some of the loughs we passed were among the most delightful I have seen. In fact darling I only needed you beside me to complete my joy. How I wish you could accompany me on a trip such as this. I feel I get all the sunshine and fun while you stay at home and do all the chores.

We arrived here at 7.45 p.m. and learned that dinner was at 8 p.m. The manager told me he was sorry the hotel was completely full, and that I would have to make do with a room full of junk. It wasn't a bedroom at all but just an old storage

201

room full of old beds, carpets, broken furniture, etc, etc. There was a comfortable bed in the room but no facilities for washing, shaving, etc. I felt snubbed and went in search of Catherwood. He was shocked when he heard about it and sent for the manager who said he could not help it. The fat was in the fire when Mrs Catherwood heard about it and particularly when she heard I was Lilla Cully's husband! He by the way knew this and told her. She was profuse in apologies and said I must get another room. There was however no way of getting another room so I had to sleep in the junk room with permission to use Catherwood's bathroom. I am to have another room tonight. The Catherwoods are genuinely sorry about the whole business and have been almost embarrassingly apologetic!

The Catherwood family have the main table in the dining room. Right at the door where he can keep his eye on the folk! A band plays during dinner and a more godless crowd would be hard to imagine. All meet in the lounge before going into dinner. Almost all have a drink before going in. I can quite imagine why Stephen Thompson says he would not come back! The Catherwood party was Mr and Mrs Catherwood and two daughters and myself. Their boy is at a Public School camp in England. All the ladies in the dining room had evening frocks and I felt a little uneasy as I was the only man without a dinner jacket. I determined however not to let this spoil a well cooked dinner, and I entered in and enjoyed the conversation at the table. I like the Catherwoods. He is just like a big boy enjoying himself running a pet hobby. The hobby is the hotel at the moment. She is a very ordinary type of person, but a good conversationalist. Whether she is playing to the gallery I know not but most of her conversation is along spiritual lines and she is well informed about missionary enterprise. He has the Chairman of British Overseas Airways Corporation staying here and is trying to arrange a special concession for missionaries using BOAC planes.

Coffee in the lounge with the Catherwoods after dinner and then a good walk along the beach with the hills of Donegal all around completed my day. I went to bed tired and slept like a log all night.

Had a good bath before breakfast and came down to enjoy a breakfast which won't help my slimming any! At breakfast Mrs Catherwood asked if I would accompany her to church this a.m. so to church I must go in the Catherwood Rolls! Often when I looked at the Catherwood Rolls Royce in Belfast I wondered what it felt like to have a ride in such a car and here I am going off to church in it with the owner's wife!

I am glad of the opportunity of coming here but I almost agree with Stephen Thompson that not much good can come out of it! However I shall know better after today! Must stop. My address at Castlerock is at Guysmere, Castlerock, Co Derry.

Cheerio darling. Love to Terence and Christopher. From your own darling husband Harry

As I delved deeper into Lilla's papers, I learned of the trials and horrors she and Harry had endured as missionaries in China. Fleeing the Japanese army, surrounded by terrified and destitute people, faith seemed to be all that kept them going through their travels.

Harry Brown and Lilla Cully met at a prayer meeting of the China Inland Mission. Both applied and were accepted to go out to China. Harry went first in 1935; Lilla joining him a couple of years later. They were married by the British Consul in Hankow in1938 and began their honeymoon at Kuling, a few miles from Hankow. As Lilla wrote, 'We occupied a palatial villa. There we stayed for a few days until suddenly the hillside was alive with rumours.'

Overnight they became refugees. Abandoning gifts and possessions, they fled with the local people through the hills and forest. Somehow they reached the mission house at Loping in Kiangsi province. As Lilla said, 'We had escaped with our lives and very little else.' In a ramshackle shelter at the Mission, Harry and Lilla set up their first home together.

Not for long. Next day the Chinese pastor in charge of the Mission sent Harry off on a six-week preaching tour. Missionary life had begun in earnest.

Three years later, Lilla found she was pregnant. In April 1942, Harry took her to Nancheng to await the birth. It was a long journey: first by launch then 70 miles overland, with Lilla in a sedan chair and Harry in a rickshaw. And they found the city was no safe haven; with the Japanese advancing and bombers overhead, they had to seek refuge in a mountain cottage.

Here, on 16th May 1942, Lilla gave birth to her first baby, Christopher Gerald. Harry cabled his family back in Northern Ireland: 'BROWNS WELL CHRISTOPHER BORN.'

On 12th June, Nancheng fell to the Japanese. The Browns were trapped: Lilla was not strong enough to walk. Yet they had to escape for the sake of the baby, and a few days later they set off on foot. They walked for eight miles, only to find their escape route cut off. They were able to rent a place to stay in a mountain village – just a room with walls on three sides and a waterproof sheet on the other. They found a Chinese umbrella to shelter the baby. Some Czech and German Catholic missionaries shared food with them, but all they could give Christopher was bean milk.

The family returned to the Mission home at Nancheng. Harry bought a cow to provide milk for the baby. But on 23rd June, the Japanese took over the city. Soldiers armed with rifles demanded to enter the Mission. They stripped Harry of his possessions: glasses, clothing… maybe next they would seize Lilla and the baby. An officer arrived. He called Harry to go with him. Harry looked at Lilla. They said goodbye. They felt sure he was to face a firing squad.

But Harry returned to his wife and child, and neither he nor they had been touched. Asked where he and Lilla came from, Harry had said 'We are both from Ireland.' And in response they were reprieved, with the words, 'Oh you poor Irish, you have suffered under the British for years.'

A few days later, Harry and Lilla were offered a chance of escape back to Loping. It would mean five days' walking over mountain tracks in blazing sun, hiding along the way as best they could and often going hungry. One day Harry went to find a post office where he could send a telegram to Mission headquarters, and met a Roman Catholic priest from northern Ireland. The priest gave him a change of clothes and some money, telling him, 'Brother, we serve a common Lord so we ought to practise a common charity.'

On the way, the baby took ill. An American doctor sent for medication, but dysentery set in, and within two days, on 3rd August at 10.50pm, Christopher died of convulsions and heat exhaustion. The Chinese watched with concern; for them the firstborn son is the greatest of all responsibilities. Harry and Lilla held a simple service, wrapped the body and left it on the hillside; there was nothing else they could have done.

Eventually, on foot and by bus, they reached Kanshein. They spent another two years with the Mission in China, preaching and surviving as best they could in broken-down huts with little food or amenity. Their daughter Rosemary and their second son Terence were born during this time, but sadly Rosemary did not survive. They wanted to take the furlough they were due, but it was difficult to arrange. Then they heard the Japanese were advancing again. Harry prayed for an aeroplane to take them to India, and asked to be put on the list for the first available flight. Next day a plane appeared. The officer in charge shouted, 'Come on, Browns! Here is God's aeroplane!'

So in 1945 they came home. The church provided them with a house in Holywood, Co Down. In 1946 a second Christopher was born: Christopher Dennis, who was to become the love of my life. The Mission wound up its operations in China, but Harry continued working for them, first as their general secretary in Northern Ireland and then covering the whole of Britain. He travelled extensively between churches and conferences, until at a Faith Mission conference in Edinburgh in 1958 he had a heart attack and died.

Arthur and Mabel Brown

Mabel met Arthur Brown in May 1942 on a boat, the Louis Pasteur, travelling to Madagascar then on to India. Mabel was a member of the Queen Alexandra's Imperial Military Nursing Service and was on her way to a posting at the 80th British General Hospital in Secunderabad. Arthur was to join his regiment, the 3rd Searchlight Battery 11th (Ulster) Light AA Regiment RA. They met at a meal onboard the ship. Afterwards they went up on deck, where she noticed that 'Paddy', as he was nicknamed, kept giving her a long look. Then he asked her to sit and talk with him. They met every day and spent the voyage getting to know each other.

They stayed for six weeks in East Africa. When Arthur sailed for India they exchanged addresses, and by the time Mabel followed he had written her lots of letters. They were married at the Cathedral of the Immaculate Conception, Secunderabad. They lived near the hospital for seven months, until Mabel was called to a hospital in Karachi and Arthur was posted to Burma. Here he heard from his mother that his brother Harry, who was a missionary in China, had escaped from the Japanese and been airlifted to Bombay. Mabel and Arthur were able to meet Harry and Lilla there.

On returning to civilian life after the war, Mabel and Arthur came back to Britain separately. For a while Mabel stayed with her parents. She and Arthur had two children, John and Fred. Although Mabel's parents were very fond of Arthur, the strictly Protestant Brown family from northern Ireland did not accept Mabel, who was Catholic, and in 1949 she and her Paddy emigrated to the USA.

Catherwood and Muriel Anderson

My own parents, Catherwood and Muriel, lived on into the 1990s. My Dad had a form of dementia, was in care, then hospital in 1992, and all his senses were closing down, but the day before he died he looked into my eyes and I knew he was saying goodbye. My mother arranged her affairs, sold her house and booked herself into an

Abbeyfield home where she was very happy. She spent Christmas day with us in 1998, enjoyed her Christmas dinner (she loved her food!), had chest pains over the next few days, was admitted to hospital for treatment but died overnight. It was very sudden but probably best for her as she needed no personal care, which she would have hated.

Chris's Australian Cousins

I kept a record when I took a trip to Australia in 2007. My relationship with John had just ended, and I was trying to get used to thinking of myself as a free independent spirit once more. But the main reasons for going were to explore the Brown side of the family, and to meet my daughter's future mother-in-law. Jenny had just become engaged to her Australian boyfriend Geoff, whose mother Marg lived in Alice Springs. Also, I had read the book, A Town Like Alice in my teens and had always wanted to visit there. My itinerary was: Belfast City Airport; London Heathrow; Singapore; Sydney, Australia; Newcastle; Sydney; Ayers Rock; Alice Springs; Sydney; Singapore; Heathrow; Belfast.

Arriving at Singapore airport, I met a lady from Glasgow called Patricia, who was en route to New Zealand for much the same reason as me. We arranged to meet at Raffles for a Singapore Sling. From my hotel sixth floor room on the same floor as the pool/gym, looking out over the pool, I walked to Raffles. Passing St Andrew's Cathedral I went in, and found a service in progress with full attendance. A fine organ, and they were singing 'Oh How I Love Jesus'. I left a Mystery Worshipper note, then shopped in Robinsons in the Raffles Centre, met Patricia and had the longed-for Sling. Chatting, I felt her life was indeed very like mine. We ate in a cheap Thai café with the locals – very hot curry with chillies! We discovered the local Chinese New Year celebrations with fireworks, and tried to find a pub. Instead we found a nice concert hall with music just finishing. Eventually, after getting lost, we had a beer in a German bar, and I got a taxi back, not feeling tired at all, so watched an ABC TV film about the baby taken by dingoes in Australia at Ayers Rock.

Next day, after a short swim in the pool, I took a taxi to the Botanical Gardens for the Tai Chi. I couldn't find it, but when I did it was just finishing, and I watched with interest. The weather being warm though overcast, I walked round the beautiful gardens, enjoying especially the orchid garden. Later, I went down to Chinatown, which was lovely, and I had an iced cappuccino at the riverfront. I headed back as heavy clouds had built up, with thunder and lightning following, and I got soaked and lost trying to get back to the hotel! Dried out and organised, I waited at the hotel entrance as arranged for Patricia, but she never arrived. Maybe she got lost too, or had a better offer! Sadly we had not exchanged details, and I never saw her again. I went to Chinatown and had baked fish and rice and a few glasses of wine, releasing a Bookcrossing book on a table. Then I felt it was time to get back and be ready for an early start. Next morning, the taxi driver gave me a full run-down on the economics of Singapore. On the plane, cruising along at 11,000 metres, 52 °C, speed 1014 KM/hour, GG mc4ch, I enjoyed the hot towels before meals, music on headphones and a video.

On arrival in Sydney, Chris's long-lost cousin Harry met me and took me on a tour of the city, and checked me into the hotel at Artimon which he had arranged. Next day, 1st March, Harry collected me and we had breakfast at his favourite cafe, the Crow's Nest, with flat whites all round, then a short drive by car and a ferry to Manly Beach where Harry had lived before and which was his favourite place. We checked out the local shops, had lunch and a walk, then back to the Crow's Nest for an Italian meal.

Next day, we walked around the beautiful Victorian shopping arcade and the Imperial Arcade, bought a book at the Tiffany Café, parking under the Sydney Harbour Bridge. Harry then drove me to nearby Newcastle, stopping briefly by a river, and I checked in at the Best Western Motel for five nights. I had an Indian meal and met with a Bookcrosser and friend I had arranged to meet at a previous Bookcrossing Convention in London.

Day three, Friday 2nd March, Harry then drove me to Lake Macquarie for lunch and toured round it a bit, then back to Newcastle for a Chinese meal at a pub, which was very good, and a swim in the hotel beforehand. Harry went to work for a while and I did some emails. He then drove me along the coast to see some great beaches. We saw two kookaburras, and had noodles at Nelson's Bay. In the evening, a meal at the Junction in a Mexican restaurant, where he fronted me about my intentions! He was not in the best of form, sneezing a bit – hay fever? I was beginning to wonder about this strange relative of my husband.

We then drove from Bowral town to Berrima, a tourist town, Georgian with cobbled streets, and Morpeth, an old port, very shabby chic! Next day, Harry arrived to say his 'hay fever' from last night was actually a bad cold, and he was still not in the best of form, but he drove me to the Source Café to meet my Bookcrossing friends and swap books. I spent an hour with them there and he took me to the beach where I read and sunbathed, then walked to Hunter St, which was completely dead, as it was Sunday afternoon. I found an internet café where I had scallops and salad and finished reading The Songlines, a book about Australian aborigine culture. Then to an internet café to email Marg, and also Jenny and Geoff, and Niall. Harry picked me up though he was still 'crook', so he just went home and I got something to eat and a bottle of wine, and had an early night.

Day six, Monday 5th March, was a trip to a winery with a small group, three French Quebecs, an Australian and myself, enjoying cheese/chutney/relish nibbles as well. There was a massive thunderstorm, but we managed to see some kangaroos. Back at 4.30, head a bit light, Harry was still not feeling well, but we drove to a restaurant on Hunter Street and had schnitzel and pasta.

Next day Harry then drove us south by the coast and explored 'Norah Head', then the seaside town of Terrigal, where we saw pelicans, and back to Sydney, where we had an Asian meal with Harry's friends in a pub, a nice group.

Day eight, Wednesday 7th, we went to the Sydney's Rocks area and had lunch there, followed by the required Sydney Opera House in the evening.

Day nine, 8th March, I took the shuttlebus to the airport and enjoyed the amazing flight to Uluru: dense urbanisation around Sydney, some rainforest, then barren desert the rest of the way. Cloudless skies, so I could see everything, and I had a great window seat (except for the wing, but that's sort of necessary!). We flew over rock formations near Uluru and saw the rock from the air. Landed in amazing heat, but with a free air-conditioned bus to the resort going round all the hotels. I sat beside a very nice guy from Denmark, who had been at a conference in Sydney but got bored with it, and left to go to the Rock instead. I later met the Danish guy again, waiting for the coach to Uluru, and gave him my copy of The Songlines. We chatted and it turned out he was a psychologist, and married.

My hotel, the Outback Pioneer, was very organised, though the room had no ensuite, only a communal toilet/washing/ showering block. I had to find the office in the shopping centre to validate my tours, but a free shuttle bus was just leaving to go around the hotels and shops, and I caught that. I had a salad at the Outback Kitchen, then a tour to Kata Tjuna, passing Ayers Rock on the way. It was very hot indeed, but I walked around the nearby gorge, and had a history and geological explanation of the area. A few comfort stops at the only toilets, one called the 'Long Drop', and it was, but at least it had a pedestal and seat, though no flush! It was then almost sunset time so our coach took us to Uluru to see the colours changing as the sun went down. Then I found I had lost my $25 entry card to the park, to be carried at all times for inspection, but had to leave the coach without it. I did need it for next day, but I managed to play it by ear. (On the sunrise tour next day, I had to pretend I had an entry card to the park, and froze every time I saw a park warden in case they did a spot check. But no one did!) As the sun went down, we had an endless supply of wine and nibbles. 'Back at the Ranch' about 8.30, I was a bit hungry, so I had a look at the BBQ. You buy your meat raw, and cook it yourself. I chose kangaroo on skewers, and one skewer of crocodile, which I got extra as he said it was a bit tough! Adding corn on the cob and a baked potato, I asked advice on how long to cook the kangaroo. I think I got it just right as it was delicious and really tender. With salads, etc. included, and another glass of wine, it was a fantastic meal, and I got to know a few people at the long trestle tables. Bed about ten, as I had an early start for the sunrise tour, and I still had to pack and check out before leaving. I slept well, but had to keep the light on as the bedside light was not working.

Day 10, I felt a bit shaky in the morning, but managed to pack and be ready for the sunrise cultural tour leaving at 6.30am. This took us to the Rock in time for the sun coming up at 7.43am. Coffee and juice were provided, and I had some nibbles. The bus then took us right around the Rock, and stopped at the Cultural Centre, where we had a proper sit-down breakfast. There I met some interesting people, including a posh lady backpacking alone. I gave her my Bookcrossing copy of A Town Like Alice. We then walked from the cultural centre to the place where people can start the climb, very steep and smooth, with no shelter from the sun. We were accompanied by an Aborigine and a translator, who told us stories and showed us how they made glue from plants, started a fire, and made spears, also how to throw a spear and carry a dish on your head.

Back at the Outback Pioneer, I got my case again, had a shower and changed into a bikini as I fancied a swim. The pool was beautiful, and I sat in the sun after to dry off. My back was blistered from the sun at Newcastle beach, and I got someone to put some cream on it, then bought a sandwich, and caught the coach to Alice Springs. Vast, flat desert all the way, straight roads with no vehicles. We changed coach at Kings Canyon, and had a comfort break at the Ebenezer Roadhouse, where I bought an ice cream, hankies and a book about boomerangs.

I arrived at Alice Springs at 6.30pm and was met by Marg, who took me to her new home where we had dinner outside with Geoff's sister Andrea. Unfortunately I felt I was developing Harry's cold. Marg's new house was beautiful and very spacious, with a nice outdoor area. I was settled into the comfy spare room with en suite, and slept well, but woke with a raw throat.

Next day, I was off with Marg toward the west, visiting Stantards, Ellory Creek and Glen Helen Gorge. Back in time to shower and change to accompany Marg to a 50th birthday party for a friend of hers called Pia, a German lady with two lovely daughters. I gave her an Irish linen handkerchief. There was a film show of still pictures of her life, a jazz band in the garden, and bring-your-own food and drink (Marg having packed champagne and a cheeseboard). She is so organised for hot weather outings, with coolbags and ice to last the day. We had had a picnic earlier, in the car as it was too hot outside, about 40 degrees!

Sunday 11th March, Marg took me to Desert Park, where we saw nocturnal species, emus, kangaroos and birds, then to the amazing hunting birds theatre, where we saw a tawny frog-mouth owl, a brown owl and a brown falcon which eats reptiles and has long legs so it can run on the ground holding the lizards away from its body. Also, a black kite which glides with translucent wings, an Australian hobby (little) falcon which relies purely on speed and agility, and whistling kites (translucent wings, but not a forked tail). Then a talk by Mark Richardson, a botanist in desert studies at Kew Gardens about a year previously. Back home again with ten minutes to pack for the airport, as we spent a while at the gift shop: socks and a boomerang for the boys and an Aussie slang book for Jenny. But no queue at the airport, and I got straight through.

Day 12, on the evening of Sunday 11th March, and Harry met me at the airport, in good form, though still showing signs of his cold. He took me back to the hotel, where I changed to go out to Chinatown in Sydney for a meal. We had a good chat, and were back at the hotel to sort out my clothes, etc. for the next few days.

Monday 12th March (Day 13), Harry drove me to Kirribilli to get a ticket for 'Derrida in Love' at the local theatre, which I had noticed was showing there (I had been reading Derrida at home before the trip). The tickets were all sold for Thursday, so I put my name on the waiting list for cancellations. Then we drove up the coast to see the northern beaches – Manly to Palm Beach, including Deewhy where his parents had lived. Back then to change for Kirribilli, and to have fish and chips.

Next day, we drove to Bowral and met some of Harry's friends, saw the Fitzroy Falls from a viewpoint, then on to the touristy village of Berrima and had pizza with Harry at Solomons.

Wednesday 14th (Day 15) Harry took me to Kirribilli to see if any tickets were available for me, but none yet, though I was the only one on the waiting list. I then met up with Jenny, a friend of Harry's, as he was off to a meeting. Jenny took me to the New South Wales Art Gallery, then Bondi Beach, and Harry drove us to Manly for a meal and half an hour on the internet at Neutral Bay, where it was very hot and sunny.

Thursday 15th March (Day 16) Harry drove me to Milson's Point and we took the train to the Darling Harbour area, had coffee in the city and walked across Pyrmont Bridge, and round Cockle Bay to the Chinese Gardens, which were very peaceful, and back via a New Age-y bookshop that Harry wanted to show me. Then back to Kirribilli, and checked again re tickets for the show, with success this time. They gave me a 'house seat' at $46 instead of $55. Harry then said goodbye to head off to Newcastle, and I set off from Kirribilli across Sydney Harbour Bridge, which was spectacular, then down through the Rocks area again to Circular Quay. I sat writing this in brilliant sunshine at the Quay, got an ice cream at Circular Quay, then walked to Hyde Park and released a Bookcrossing book about SE Australia. I walked up to Town Hall station, calling into St Andrew's Cathedral on the way, got a train to St Leonards, then a bus to the hotel, a pizza at the bus stop, and back to change for the theatre that evening. The taxi was late and I had to hail one instead. The play was brilliant, but the taxi cost $18.50, and I was worried I might not have enough change for the taxi back, which would cost more after ten, but I really wanted a drink at the interval. So I asked the barman if I could use my card, to which he replied no, but when I said I was short as I was leaving for the UK the next day, he gave me a glass of champagne on the house! I got another $20 from a machine anyway, and the taxi was just $20 (£8).

Final day, Friday 16th March (Day 17) I woke early as I had left my phone on and it rang at 4.45am. I pressed Yes, and couldn't sleep again, so was up and ready far too soon. But I thought it would make me tired later and I might sleep on the plane. I would be home again in 26 hours plus the time difference (35 hours) plus five hours at Singapore and five at Heathrow.

What an amazing trip! And so pleased to have met with a relative from Chris's past. This family tree hobby was so interesting. Or so I thought! On my return, I had a really nasty email from Harry, saying he had considered I was an introvert with no interest in anything but the internet, and he would not be in touch anymore. Ah well, c'est la vie! Next day was my birthday. I felt his email said more about him than about me, and let it go.

After some years without further correspondence with the Australian members of the Brown family, cousin Steve came over to Northern Ireland in 2018 to research his Anderson connections.

The McCoubreys of New York

There was a less-than-delightful follow-up to my research on the McCoubreys at Clough. The story began when I was contacted on Facebook by an American who claimed she was related to me from way back in our combined family history. She was coming to Ireland on family history research and wanted to meet with me. I was delighted, as researching my family tree is one of my main hobbies. In due course, she and her husband arrived, and the sleepy village of Clough was added to one of my new places to visit. Of course, they were enchanted with northern Ireland, and before they left, invited me to visit them in New York. This got added to my bucket list, and I thought about it only occasionally. But before long they were asking me again, saying they would be organising a Meeting of the

216

Clans, with me as the main guest! I was tempted, and taking my courage in both hands, I agreed and booked my flights for the end of May, when the weather would be warming up. Emails flew back and forth, organising my itinerary while there. The ESTA form was completed and the flights booked from Dublin to JFK. The itinerary included driving north of New York State to see the town my ancestors had settled in and where they were buried. My excitement was rising, but I was worried about a pain in my right thigh that was getting worse.

Anyway, I started getting my clothing sorted for the trip, and carried on with life as well as I could, until at a cinema trip with my U3A group, I knew I would not be able to walk from the cinema to the train station. I took a taxi home. It was about a week before I was due to fly to New York, and I had started packing. My leg hurt so badly, I ran a hot bath and allowed the water to ease the pain. And then it happened. I rose to get out, swung one leg onto the floor and went to lift the other one. Splash! I was back in the water. I had heard a crack, and knew immediately something was very wrong. I could not even try to get out of the bath on my own, and the realisation began to dawn on me that something really bad had happened. And the holiday was just a week away! Being a sensible sort of girl, I normally take my mobile into the bathroom, so it seemed the only option was to ring 999 and explain the situation. They agreed I probably needed an ambulance, so I lay in the warm water, wondering what had happened, and whether I would get to New York. I called a doctor friend for help, telling her the story, and how to get into the house using the key in the key box outside the front door. She soon arrived with a friend, but unfortunately I had left the key on the inside of the lock. Soon the ambulance crew arrived. I gave them the name of the company that had fitted the locks, and they at last gained entry.

The rest was quite hilarious, as I had to be lifted dripping and naked out of the bath on a towel. The bathroom door had to be removed, and soon I was in the ambulance, heading for the Royal. My friends found nightwear and toiletries, and I could not believe this was all happening! Next stop, X-ray, and a question I wasn't expecting. 'Have you been taking alendronic acid for osteoporosis of your bones?' 'Yes!' 'How long?' 'Eight years.' 'Well, you have a fractured femur, caused by taking that medication for longer than five years.'

I was operated on that morning, and was in hospital for three weeks. The New York trip was cancelled along with the offending medication, and the insurance paid up in due course. And in 2017, I finally did the trip to Long Island for an amazing 'Gathering of the Clans', seeing President Roosevelt's home, Trump Tower, Times Square, the 9/11 memorial, the Flatiron building and a musical, and finally the trip north to where my McCoubrey ancestors had settled and were buried.

To bring the family tree up to date, here are my entries on my own career and my three children.

My Work

Having trained as a nurse in 1967, I continued working in another hospital until Jenny was born in 1972, and afterwards as a Marie Curie nurse until 1981 when Jonathan was born. With Chris's illness and death I ceased regular work, as his life insurance provided enough for us to live on. While the children were young, I did some work in local nursing homes and a girls school, and volunteered on local schools' boards of governors until 1992. At this point I enrolled in a back-to-nursing course, where the tutors advised that due to my worsening arthritis I should look for work in education or research.

After this I worked part time as a practice nurse, until I got a job in the Royal Victoria Hospital Belfast metabolic department as a Clinical research nurse. I retired in 2009.

My Children

I am intensely proud of all my children, each for different reasons, for they are all extremely different. People say that Jenny and Jonathan have Chris's looks, but I think Niall has his personality - his calm, logical way of looking at things, his intense interest in small detail, and of course, his ability in electronics. Jenny also has his business sense, and Jonathan his sense of adventure. Home computers were just coming on the scene when Chris died, and we bought a Commodore 64 as soon as the kids could start to learn, and have had a working computer ever since. Babysitters had to have an interest in physics and electronics to help me nurture the growing computer skills and electronic circuit-board production. I would come back to find bits of wire all over the floor! I know Chris would be proud to see all three of his children going on in the computer scene.

Jenny Rachel

Happily married since 1969, Chris and I decided to start a family. Unfortunately our first pregnancy ended at 20 weeks with a miscarriage. As a nurse, I knew that this often happened with a first pregnancy, and it did not concern us too much. For me it confirmed that I was able to get pregnant, and we went on trying. I was working as a part-time staff nurse at the Ulster Hospital, just across the road from where we lived. Next time the pregnancy went well, and on 17th August 1972 I was admitted to that same hospital pending delivery. Unfortunately, it was a difficult birth. The baby was

219

presenting 'face to pubes' which meant either a forceps delivery or Caesarean section. From memory it seemed there was no one available to perform a CS, so forceps delivery was the only option. It was painful, the doctor having to advise me that if I didn't keep still, he might harm the baby! But eventually she was born, that curious, strong-minded girl who has over the years brought me both joy and pain!

As a small child, Jenny was bright, friendly and very eager to learn. Visiting the doctor's surgery at about age four, she would chat to the other patients, asking them if they'd like a magazine to read! Having an August birthday, she started primary school already aged five and did well. Previous to that she attended the local kindergarten run by Mrs Friers, the wife of a local artist, and having tried all the toys there, and not yet old enough to start 'big' school, she had a year at the newly opened Steiner School nursery class, where she developed her artistic side. At her interview for Holywood Primary School, the renowned Miss Beacom declared Jenny Brown would do well in life. Bright and bubbly, she made friends and loved birthday parties, out-of-school ballet classes, gymnastics, dressing up and horse riding. But her happy childhood was cut short with the sudden death of her beloved Dad. She seemed to cope at first as well as possible. She passed her 11+, though she came out in a nervous rash while awaiting her results, and went on to Upper Sullivan, her father's school. But on entering her teens, she went through a 'gothic' stage. She refused to go to church as she announced she didn't believe in God, and became a difficult and rebellious teenager. Unsurprising probably, as we were all learning to cope without a beloved husband and Dad. She couldn't wait to get away from home, and chose Liverpool University for her next stage of education. This didn't work out and she got a place at Manchester Metropolitan University instead to do a European Studies degree, which she passed with a 2-2. There were of course boyfriends and many heartbreaks. As a single parent I could not always be there for her in England when she was deeply upset by these, though her Aunt Sue from Dublin often filled that gap. As a result, I seemed to be the enemy, and blamed for many things.

Jenny enjoyed a part-time job with Habitat, later spending some time at their Exeter and Belfast branches, and it provided an outlet for her artistic talent. Her next job was as a medical rep, then a recruitment consultant with EA Games near London (fulfilling her great ambition of moving to London), and eventually recruitment consultant for Google, where she still works and which she still enjoys. At that time she met her husband, Geoff, thankfully an excellent choice, an Australian dentist living in Richmond, Surrey. She shared his tiny basement flat on Richmond Hill, which happened to be next door to one of Mick Jagger's houses. Jenny and Geoff were married in Richmond Registry Office, followed by a huge event in a nearby pub with all their friends. Children followed, helped by several attempts at IVF. Imogen, my first grandchild, was a source of great delight, and they continued living at the beautiful Richmond Hill flat until Jenny was pregnant with twins, when they realised a bigger home was needed.

Again they were fortunate (with some help from the bank of Mum and Dad) to get a beautiful home, this time in Twickenham, a house which had been derelict for years until a developer bought it, gutted the inside and produced a modern five-bedroomed home with small gardens front and rear and room to park a car. Geoff was still able to travel to his surgery in Richmond by bike or scooter, and there they still are. Jenny is a wonderful Mum to Imogen, Astrid and Aurora, and a joy to visit, despite her heartfelt belief that any problem can be solved just by googling it: Google is now her God!

But being her mother is not always easy.

Around this time, my arthritis was causing me more problems, with knees and hands becoming stiff and painful, so stairs, toilets and bedside light switches were a problem. I had been diagnosed with arthritis by a friendly rheumatologist back in 1980. It had flared up from time to time, including after Jonathan was weaned in 1982 and around the time Chris died. Although medical treatment had kept the arthritis more or less under control, there were times when I admitted I was 'in agony'. I had difficulty convincing Jenny what I meant without seeming to whine. I bought a rollator to help with the long walks in London, though Jenny thoughtfully but prematurely bought me a wheelchair. I loved seeing her daughters grow up and visited about twice a year, or occasionally Jenny would travel to northern Ireland with one child, giving her special time, and this seemed to work well. However, over the years things became more difficult between us, with mounting frustration on my side and impatience on hers, as I was not as able as her mother-in-law to help with the children. I always feel Jenny has never stopped missing her father and I could never take his place. I started visiting for shorter periods, though of course I continue to see them regularly, and will do so for as long as I can. Jenny and Geoff were both working full time with help from an au pair and cleaner, so life was quite stressful for them. It was very different to my life as a mother, when I had not needed to work until my children went to school.

A blog entry from February 2018 describes a trip to Iceland with my daughter Jenny and grand-daughter Aurora:

A long-time bucket list item rose to the top recently, when I noticed that Icelandair were now flying from Belfast, the little airport 15 minutes from my home. The local travel agent had a package for February, and I was just about to book it when

I mentioned it to my daughter in London. The response was 'We want to go too!' meaning my daughter and grand-daughter, named appropriately Aurora. But I'm flying from Belfast! Package abandoned, and much scurrying about the internet as we tried to source appropriate flights. A friend says she knows someone who specialises in packages to Iceland. Daughter considers it rather expensive and persuades me to do separate flights, and she would get a place to sleep using the Internet. Iceland specialist offers to arrange trips while we are there to suit my ageing inability to walk long distances or climb steep steps into coaches, and daughter agrees. I pay for all flights and the Iceland package, leaving food shopping and eating out to daughter, as these happen. As February approaches, my husband Paul, in care with dementia, is admitted to hospital with pneumonia. Cancellation considered, but he conveniently passes away four-five weeks before the trip. I'm sad, but relieved his Alzheimer's journey is over. All good considering, funeral over, visitors away, legal paperwork begun, packing commenced, and Iceland becomes my post-traumatic respite holiday. Paul would have said, 'You go!!' He used to call ME Bossy Boots! Thank you, Paul!

Our flights would arrive about an hour apart, and our driver Olav would collect us both, and drive to the Blue Lagoon for our first Icelandic experience before dropping us off at the 'Ice Apartments'. On the morning we are due to leave, my daughter texts that her flight is cancelled. Frantic attempts to rebook with another airport produce a result. I take a taxi to my local airport, ETD 10am, and as we approach the airport my taxi driver says my plane is delayed. Checking in, it will leave at 6pm. Snow is starting to fall as I settle in for the long wait, relax buying duty-free wine, cosmetics, and availing of a free facial. By 7.30 I'm in the air, and three hours later arrive in a severe blizzard. The Blue Lagoon, as previously arranged for that day, was now out of the question. My daughter texts to say they can't even get into the accommodation, so I book a night in another guest house. My driver negotiates expertly through increasing snowfall, we find accommodation two and settle for the night. Next day, the driver collects us, complete with all bags and my walker and we arrive at accommodation one, negotiating badly parked cars blocking our entrance way. Then I went with my daughter to discuss the previous night's access problem with the owner of the apartment next day, and we settle ourselves, exhausted and stressed, in the very welcome and cosy beds.

Next morning we head off with our driver on the arranged plan to the Golden Circle, on snowy roads, visiting the Thingvellir National Park, and stopping at the Secret Lagoon for a swim in the geothermal heated water. Amazingly we encounter many cars that have accidentally driven off the edge of the road, probably tourists in hire cars, according to Olav. Lunch at the Farmers Cafe overlooking the cows munching at their hay, we enjoy an excellent Icelandic lamb dinner, and head off in the deepening snow for a photoshoot at the Gulfoss waterfall and see a geyser erupt at Strokkur.

Plan for next day is to talk to the accommodation admin in the nearby shop, which proves difficult to locate, and we explore the local shops, have coffee, see the tall church and enjoy an Icelandic Pancake Day treat for lunch. With the apartment admin eventually located, it appears I have not forwarded to my daughter an email explaining late access to the apartment. The email arrived the day after my husband's death and was thus off my radar. My daughter hurls abuse at my poor email review management as she is embarrassed, but negotiates a 50% reduction on the first night. This has not appeared in my bank, but I put it down to bereavement expenses.

Our last full day is to drive to the south coast. Olav has brought his eight-year-old daughter as company for Aurora. It is snowing hard, and he suggests a city tour seeing interesting sites, walking on the frozen Pond, a visit to the Whale Museum, and lunch in the Perlan restaurant overlooking the city. It's still snowing hard and roads to the south have been closed. Jenny suggests snowboarding for the kids, and Olav helpfully finds a suitable hill, having thoughtfully packed boards in the boot of his four-wheel drive. We join the queue of cars waiting to drive south, it's getting dark, but we eventually make it, driving again through snow-clad high mountains, and find a delightful restaurant where we enjoy welcome Icelandic fare. And the day ends on a high note, as we stop at a place Olav knows is good for watching the Northern Lights. We are not disappointed, and Olav parks in a dark spot for us to enjoy the amazing treat we had come to see, the Aurora Borealis.

Our journey home was thankfully less eventful, and we can look back on a holiday never to be forgotten.

Niall

Niall was born on 30th January 1976, and it was snowing the day he arrived. I had a dreadful cold, and when people asked what his name would be, they were told 'Diall'! He was born seven years after the 'Troubles' began in Northern Ireland. Perhaps we were at that point in our lives where we wanted to make a statement about where we stood. 'Niall of the Nine Hostages' was a semi-mythical High King of Ulster, and as such, this choice proclaimed both our Irishness and our Ulsterness. We were also at a stage where we were reexamining the necessity of various things that tended to be taken for granted, like Middle Names, which Chris felt were just a nuisance, were never used, and nobody ever liked. And anyway, there was no other name we agreed on!

Although Niall was just six years old when his Dad died, he always seemed to feel that he was the man of the house, ready with his tools to fix anything his Mum couldn't manage. It has been a real joy for me to see him grow up and away, maturing physically, emotionally and spiritually, learning life skills at Scouts and putting them into practice as he moved away from home, first to a bible course in Estonia for six months, and then to Edinburgh University. I was happy for him in his first choice of partner, a Scottish student called Jenni, whom he met and married at university in 1997, but sad that Chris was not there at his wedding too, though in some sense he was. He was there in me, in my memories, and in my heart, and most of all, he was there in my children. Niall and Jenni were both keen Christians. I enjoyed getting to know Jenni, and felt she would support him in all his plans for the future, and that theirs would be a good and equal partnership in the working out of those plans. Even back then, 21 was quite a young age to get married, and Niall's Uncle Terence and I both advised them to wait a while before marrying. But they wouldn't wait, and seeing their point of view I congratulated them on flouting the convention to marry late. A 'young' wedding meant a modern wedding, and it gave me great pleasure to see them put their own stamp on the actual ceremony, showing their own individual commitment to God and to each other. They had my blessing as they started out on their married life together, and I loved the way we sang at the wedding ceremony about God delighting in his children as I delighted in mine.

226

Sadly, it was not to last. After a short few years together, Jenni left Niall to pursue her interests alone. I was devastated, and so was Niall, to the extent that sadly he relinquished his faith in the God they had felt had led them together, only to tear them apart. It was sad for us all that after just four years, they decided to separate. Together they attended a friend's wedding in Paris in 2001, and there said their goodbyes. They were divorced in 2003. (This was my annus horribilis, when Jonathan dropped out of his university course and Jenny had an early pregnancy termination). Niall decided to take time out and went to teach English as a foreign language in Prague. Here he was to meet Barbora, who in 2007 became his new wife, and go on to have two delightful boys: Matthew and Toby. He now works there as an engineer, designing components for cars and mobile phones. Unfortunately, as he is paid from a Scottish company, his income has gone down due to the uncertainty over Brexit. However, they plan to live there and Bara, who trained as an architect, has started a home business selling house paraphernalia online. I visit most years, enjoying the summer heat and occasionally the Christmas cold weather.

Jonathan Patrick

Jonathan was our 'late' one. We had always wanted a third child, but it didn't seem to happen when planned, and as always in these situations, as soon as we relaxed about it, it happened! But as he was only 14 months old when his father died, he has no memory of Chris, his father. As a small child he would have temper tantrums and hold his breath if he did not get his way, and as an adult he was his father's double in looks, though less so in personality. The older ones enjoyed having a younger brother to tease and he took it in good sport. However, as he had a June birthday, his progress was always behind that of his older classmates. During his last years in primary school, his class teacher was absent a lot as she had cancer, so he made particularly slow progress, especially in reading. His 11-plus results were not good enough to get a place in the grammar school his siblings attended, and I had to pay for him to attend a fee-paying school for a year, which he hated. But the following year he got a place in the local school, where he did well, apart from frequent detentions for being late and once attempting to blow up the science lab!

Jonathan was an easy-going child, but became somewhat obsessive and fastidious as he grew older. He seemed to have little social life, preferring to stay in his room alone listening to pop music – mostly Oasis – and trying to create video games on his computer. However, he achieved good grades and went on to Edinburgh University to study computer science. While Jenny had received a grant and Niall a bursary at university, Jonathan had a loan as the government had cut back on student funding. At age 18 he received a sum from his father's will as he had the others, but soon spent the lot, and I perhaps foolishly gave him use of my credit card, which was soon overdrawn. Even though he had received a student loan, I paid his lodgings bill. He found living in a group flat difficult, and after a couple of years he tried to drop out. His brother and sister managed to persuade him to return, unknown to me. He then asked for a year out and came home to the flat I had moved to. (I had decided it was time to downsize from the six-bedroom terrace we had enjoyed but was becoming expensive to maintain). At the flat, he slept in late and worked late in his room on a video game, which never seemed to come to anything. People thought he would make a fortune with it, but as he was not paying rent to me I suggested getting a part-time job as a waiter. This did not work and he became quite unsocial and difficult. When the time came to return to studying, he said he had spoken to the university and was not returning. I began to suspect he might have a form of Asperger's Syndrome, and asked the GP to investigate. But the doctor just asked, 'Does he wash?' 'Yes, to an extreme, and refuses to have his clothes washed with mine!' When I approached Jonathan about the possibility of Asperger's, he flew into a rage and would not discuss it.

Eventually he moved out to Belfast, then Germany, Amsterdam and Australia, but kept in touch, visiting me and his siblings occasionally. The last time he stayed with me, after I had remarried and moved house, he had a bout of flu and stayed in his room the whole time. This happened again at his brother's home. Sometimes he asked me for small amounts of money, and as I had loaned the others money towards new houses, I agreed to some small loans. But they were never returned. He then moved to Vietnam and gave me an address which turned out to be a backpackers' hostel. His post still came to my home but he had asked me to just forward it and never to open it.

This went on for a few years, until in 2015 he asked me to meet him in Bali. I booked the holiday, but unfortunately my husband Paul, who was in care by then with Alzheimer's, was taken to hospital with a suspected heart attack and I had to cancel. Jonathan said he understood, but from that time he never answered my emails, and none of us have heard from him since 2016. We phoned the backpackers' hostel to be told he had moved in with a girlfriend. I started opening his letters and found he was in debt and was not replying to the bank, who of course would not discuss it with me. He had already unfriended me and his siblings on Facebook, so his website was the only way we could check if he was even alive! There were a few photos of him socialising with a local girl, and some videos on Youtube show him doing presentations on virtual currency, where he looked well and seemed happy. I paid his debt to near the amount I had given his siblings, but he did not acknowledge it. As far as I know, he works for Ethereum and uses bitcoins, and these seem to dominate his life. I would consider going to look for him, but don't think I could bear the chance of not finding him. Instead, I write him emails that remain unanswered.

Muriel's sister Doris

Three Brown brothers: Herbert, Bob and Arthur

Sixmilecross, where my Anderson grandmother was born

Susanna Bell, my Anderson grandmother from County Tyrone

My grandmother Norah after whom I was named

My brother Arthur, with his wife and my brother in law Terence Brown at Jenny's wedding

Three great kids of mine!

Jenny's family in London

Trannarossan

8
EMBRACING THE CRACKS IN LIFE

Yes, I'm a pragmatist, embracing the cracks in life that make us who we are. A recent Radio 4 programme talked about this, stating, 'There is nothing more whole than a broken heart', and, 'It is the cracks that let the light in'. I am a fragile bird that can still fly, a 'blackbird singing in the dead of night'.

The last question my mother asked me before she died was, 'Are you still an Evangelical?'

She had reason to doubt my commitment. Evangelism means different things to different people, and her definition may not have been exactly the same as mine. Hers may have been closer to fundamentalism, whereas I would call myself 'post-evangelical'. Well before I got involved with Corrymeela and all it represented for the fractured communities of northern Ireland, I was asking questions about how and why Christianity could seem to do two things at once: bring people together and divide them.

Some Christianity-related words need explaining, though a glance at the Oxford English Dictionary shows how widely their interpretations may vary. 'Fundamentalists' believe every word of the Bible is divinely inspired and therefore true (though the word can also be used of those who hold strictly to the fundamental principles of any set of beliefs). 'Evangelical' can mean simply 'based upon or following from the Gospels', but often denotes particular Protestant denominations that emphasise the need to attain salvation through faith alone in Christ's atonement. 'Post-evangelical' Christians dissociate themselves from more traditional evangelical churches, which they perceive as narrow-minded and resistant to various aspects of today's society, such as developments in science, trends in the arts, and our general multicultural outlook. Also, they feel the Bible is often read in the context of today, whereas it was written in relation to a very different time, and there has been some incorrect translation from early original documents.

I feel terms such as 'ecumenical', 'charismatic' and 'latitudinarian' are more to do with agendas than with faith or belief. One can be a Christian and include all or some of them, according to the weight of importance one attaches to each. Some years earlier, my mother told me she had come to the conclusion that I was guilty of latitudinarianism. She sent me a note which stated: 'You need to watch you do not get more hooked on Christendom than on the Church, which is composed of all true believers.' I think she was probably right in saying I was latitudinarian, though I didn't quite get the difference she implied between the Church and Christendom.

I had been brought up in the very evangelical Christian Brethren, whose sole purpose seemed to me to influence people to be 'saved', i.e. you must commit to trusting in the Lord Jesus to give complete security in an afterlife in heaven by renouncing all sin and following his teachings. As for following the teachings of Christ, I was totally in favour of that. But I never quite got my head around the idea of sin, as I was a very innocent child and would never have performed any actions that went against the Ten Commandments. However, in my heart I wondered why smoking, alcohol, make-up, dancing, theatre, ballet, cinema, trousers on girls, even divorce, might be classed together as 'sin'. The one tenet I did cling to was that sex before marriage must be wrong because having sex implied total commitment. In later years I came to reconsider that matter more closely!

But having been 'saved' at the tender age of seven, I could see that there were good points to this whole Christian thing:

1. It gave me a life structure for growing up.

2. It kept my parents and relatives happy.

3. In my childish head it seemed to make some sort of sense.

I began to ask more questions when I moved from a local 'paid-for' prep school to the nearby primary school. Here I met a wonderful teacher who, although she was Presbyterian, read from the same Bible as we did, and even taught the same hymns. But our Brethren Sunday School teachers taught me that Presbyterians might not be saved, and that they might sin by wearing make-up or going to the theatre or cinema. Questions started forming in my mind, but I never discussed these with my parents as around this time my mother was suffering recurrent 'nervous breakdowns', which were often triggered by something happening which she did not agree with. So I kept my questions to myself. I was very aware when I moved school that practically all the other pupils were Presbyterian or Anglican, and I did feel quite isolated being marked as 'Brethren', which no one else seemed to be. I just wished I could be the same as the others!

Moving on to grammar school at the age of 12, having passed my 'qualifying exam' or 11+, I found a whole new world of thought. Some of the girls (it was an all-girls school) even swore (loudly!), which in my innocent way I was at first shocked about, but soon realised it did no harm and could easily be ignored. The school had an Anglican ethos, ie. it was Christian, but definitely not 'evangelical'. There was a Scripture Union after-school club, which of course I attended regularly. My parents approved of this without even knowing what it was like: its name just fitted the box they expected me to be put in. The teacher in charge of Scripture Union was fairly casual about how she approached it: Bible reading was important but there were no threats of hell, or expectations about modest clothing, or disapproval of leisure activities like the cinema or theatre. These activities were counted as normal. I also had a penpal from Romford in Essex who, when I said I was a Christian, said she was too. But when we discussed this, her definition seemed very different to mine. You can understand how my young and growing mind was becoming somewhat confused. School assembly was another anachronism: we sang the same hymns (but with less sincerity I thought), and recited the Lord's Prayer daily without much thought about what it meant.

An early lightbulb moment for me was as a young teenager, when I was unable to avoid taking part in a cold door-knocking session in Belfast. We had to proclaim the gospel on doorsteps and try to convince people there and then to commit to the message of Jesus. I didn't like the moment when pressure had to be used, and ever since I have despised cold calling in any situation. I now believe people should have the right to make decisions independently, and especially the path their spiritual life should follow.

At weekends, with some friends from 'the meeting' or 'the hall' as our church was called, I joined 'Help Heavenward', a teenage-geared Saturday evening group, where I thought I would be able to discuss some of my rising questions. It felt very grown-up at first, but soon I realised my questions seemed either inappropriate or produced an answer I did not agree with. Sex was such a hidden subject, and we were all so afraid of perhaps getting caught kissing or even holding hands (which I would have dearly liked to try), that it was never even discussed. All I had to go on was the booklet my mother gave me when my periods started: a Family Doctor book about fruit-flies! And the advice to never discuss periods with boys or even (especially) my father!

Then a new outlet appeared at the YMCA on a Saturday night: 'The Rendezvous'. This was a Christian but interdenominational young people's meeting, with eminent Christian speakers who approached subjects such as 'sex and marriage'. I was hopeful at first, but again it seemed to me to toe the line just as my own church group did. But it was a way to meet other young people, and I became quite enthusiastic, attending early-morning prayer meetings before school as well as after-school events with some more interesting speakers. My social life was beginning to speed up: my friends and I would go for a coffee at a nearby cafe before or after the service, and start to meet boys from other churches. Other girls were getting boyfriends, but I was too shy to make the right moves. I still had a long way to go before I met anyone, either male or female, who agreed with my thoughts. I just remember having one conversation with some Brethren girlfriends about boys, and whether it would be OK to go out with a boy who 'wasn't a Christian'. I don't think anyone was brave enough to say it was! It was beginning to seem to me that life would become incredibly dull if I stayed with the Brethren.

I find a note to myself (from CWR?) stating 'Right Belief': 'In Christ I am adequate to handle all the responsibilities God gives me.' (Underneath in childish handwriting, the hurtful comment, 'You never did A-levels,' and on the back the space for 'Wrong Belief' is empty.)

Certain books later helped me get my thoughts in order:

•The Road Less Travelled by M. Scott Peck – about the nature of loving relationships and gaining self-knowledge through dealing with our problems

- Doubt by Os Guinness – on understanding and overcoming Christian doubt

- The Call to Commitment by Jim Wallis of Sojourners, a Christian body in America. I had met Jim while in Corrymeela. He, like me, was brought up in the Brethren, and I liked what he wrote.

- Books by Brian McLaren and Karen Armstrong (The Case for God)

- The Post Evangelical by Dave Tomlinson, which influenced me greatly. These were the essentials I abstracted from it:

- Evangelicals have an appetite for theology. However, they face the danger of assuming as an absolute truth their own particular notion of what is essential to the Christian faith.

- Middleclass values form the dominant cultural norm in most evangelical churches, which identify Christianity with the standards, values and attitudes of their own culture.

- Much religious language is vacuous, but the way we use it develops through four stages as we come to think more deeply:

Stage 1: Self-obsessed

Stage 2: Conformist (assuming God to be transcendent and judgemental)

Stage 3: Individualistic (sceptic, doubting, questioning)

Stage 4: Integrated (a more intuitive sense of wholeness, including acceptance of what cannot be fully grasped yet is still to be sought).

So where do I stand in this? Here I am, born into this community (the Brethren), characterised by distrust and suspicion. But as the eldest child of a generation I grow up with an aura of specialness, an expectation of hope for the future, loved with an intensity made stronger by the shared faith of new parents (mine) who believe as their parents (my grandparents) did, but also from a generation whose own parents had rejected their traditional and perhaps stifling upbringing in the more established church patterns of

Presbyterianism and church liturgy. Is there a questioning gene that leapfrogs generations? Why did I, at an early age, question everything, though discouraged from doing so? Is it a 'thranness' so often found in this community?

Although my faith continued as strongly as ever throughout the years I was growing up, getting married and then raising my children, I came to adopt a much broader outlook and was much readier to consider other opinions than during my early years among the Brethren.

And yet my faith still holds, though growing weak at times, but returning as I get older. My faith is summed up in a quotation from Rev John Stott: 'The purpose of the Gospel is not salvation, but fellowship (with God and other Christians). I John I v.3. And the ultimate purpose is the completion of joy!'

It is now over 20 years since I wrote the chapter about losing Chris, and I admit that my relationship towards God changed as the children grew up and eventually left home. I was grateful to Chris and also to God for the financial provision I received, but at times I was despairing as I tried to manage the teenage years on my own, and this affected my faith. I joined a semi-religious group called Ikon, which was composed mainly of younger arty people also going through their own questioning, but still holding on to a faith of sorts. They helped me cope with this time of doubt and questioning. I still attended church, but this was mainly to enjoy the music, as my more liberal views on faith and local sectarianism were not always accepted. I eventually left the Presbyterian church, only meeting with the Ikon group or attending Corrymeela events, and occasionally attending the Church of England, where we were married, with my second husband Paul. Then on returning to northern Ireland in 2010 we joined the Non-Subscribing Presbyterian

Church, which has a more liberal viewpoint and where I now feel more at home.

Corrymeela and Being a Presbyterian Peace Agent, 1987-1999

Corrymeela is all about peace and reconciliation. It started in 1965 when Ray Davey, a chaplain in Belfast, gathered a group of students from Queen's University to discuss their concern over the tensions brewing in Northern Ireland between different political and religious ideologies. As a prisoner of war in Dresden in 1945, Ray had witnessed the bombing of the city, and the experience had changed his life. His mission to bring people together to promote understanding and tolerance took shape in the Corrymeela community, 'an open village for all people of good will'. Throughout the Troubles of the 1970s and 80s, Corrymeela gathered together people of different political and religious outlook, and these days it addresses strife and division anywhere in the world. Its residential centre is up on the beautiful headland near Ballycastle in Co Antrim.

I first visited Corrymeela with Chris when Jenny was a baby, and later became involved sometime after Chris's death when a friend, Jean Boyd, mentioned a new event taking place at Corrymeela as a sort of summer school: it was called Summerfest and combined a festival of outdoor and children's activities with discussion groups and worship. When I looked at the programme, I thought it sounded so interesting and stimulating that I decided to take the children there for part of their summer holidays, and we carried on doing so for several years. Later I became a 'Friend' of Corrymeela, and also attended 'Adult Seed Groups', a Pilgrims Way weekend and an Enneagram weekend. I have been able to apply the ideas generated there to church work and other areas of life. Later I joined the Corrymeela Singers, until they disbanded and a new choir called Voices Together was formed, of which I am still a member.

Following the Troubles of the 1970s, the long complicated process of rebuilding communities fell partly to the churches. The Presbyterian church appointed congregational peace agents – volunteers who would look for opportunities to mix with representatives from other denominations and organise activities that would bring congregations together. When my church advertised the role, I applied eagerly, because I felt my experience with Corrymeela would enable me to make a worthwhile contribution.

But someone else was given the post. I was disappointed, as I felt I could have been useful in that sort of work, and the person appointed did not carry through on the opportunities I could see. Later, I joined another congregation in the area, Ballygilbert Presbyterian Church, and was after all asked to be their peace agent. I was glad to accept. This congregation had already formed a connection with St Agnes' Catholic Church on the Falls Road, and needed a person willing to continue organising joint events in both churches. Inspired by the work they were already doing, I undertook the job during the years 1990-99. A very nice lady at St Agnes' gave me the name 'Peaceangel' for being a peace agent, and I later used this as my Bookcrossing name. In 1997 I was co-opted onto the Ards Presbytery Community Relations Committee for two years and worked with deep enthusiasm, also attending several ECONI (Evangelical Contribution on Northern Ireland) events.

The regular events organised between St Agnes and Ballygilbert Presbyterian continued for many years, and good relationships developed between members of both churches. An enthusiastic group regularly attended joint events for special services and friendship outings. However, over time the group grew smaller, because those attending had already been involved for many years, and some including myself were growing older and had health problems. At this point, I became aware of a project in the Presbyterian Church: 'Preparing Youth for Peace'. I felt this could offer a solution for our group. I approached the youth leader in the church, who seemed interested but did not follow up on my suggestion. After a time I mentioned this to the minister, but still nothing happened. As I felt this was important and the numbers in our group were continuing to drop due to age and infirmity, I approached the Church Session. But my suggestion was ignored. My own health was a problem at the time, and I felt I should resign. Disillusioned, I later left Ballygilbert Presbyterian Church. But as a peace agent around that time, I was honoured to be invited with the minister of Ballygilbert and my current partner John to attend a formal dinner at Aras an Uachtarain, the home of the Irish President, who was then Mary McAleese. While I was travelling in England I attended Church of England services, and on my return to northern Ireland re-considered the situation.

Philip Orr's article for the Centre for Contemporary Christianity in Ireland, Christianity with Medium Fries, rang bells for me as I had become increasingly concerned about the direction of change in churches today. Orr argued that contemporary Christianity ran the risk of being sucked into the McDonald's business model, where evangelism was aimed at 'a consumer society accustomed to experiencing religion as lifestyle and product'. The McDonald's model offered instant gratification for the consumer (ie churchgoer); a highly regulated customer experience you could be sure would be the same in every town; and rapid business growth. In the Church, this tended to translate into happy-clappy gatherings; bestselling paperbacks of the 'find Jesus and change your life in five easy steps' type; formulaic scripts for every sermon, as in the Alpha course; a race between ministers to fill up the pews with converts.

Not that I was against change per se; on the contrary, I embraced change as often as possible. Considering how Jesus applied a different approach to each person he met, I felt conversion was nowadays made too simplistic, designed to fit a certain mould. Alpha course leaders expected you to agree with all that was stated and discussed afterwards. Easy-listening worship songs especially reduced the depth of spiritual experience – I was comparing them to the sublime inspiration I found through singing sacred music. As I wrote in response to Philip Orr, American models for church growth were indeed too much influenced by the McDonald's model.

Although I was prepared to work hard for my Christian community, I had never been happy about the need to agree to the Westminster Confession of Faith (the set of doctrines adopted by most Protestant sects in Britain in the 17th century, and intended to unite them) and concluded that I would never consent to being an elder in the traditional Presbyterian Church. Looking at the Non-Subscribing Presbyterian Church, I felt I could be more at ease there. I was interested in its history and theology, and I felt I was being drawn back to my roots. I first attended the Non-Subscribing Presbyterian church at Holywood as a mystery-worshipper, leaving a form admitting I would consider making it my church. I did in fact join, more on account of gut feeling than anything else, but also knowing what they were not subscribing to – the Westminster Confession of Faith!

Shortly afterwards, I was approached through Facebook by an American lady who thought we might be related. It turned out we both had ancestors called McCoubrey, who were buried in the graveyard at Clough Non-Subscribing Presbyterian Church (as mentioned in the Family Tree chapter). I found I had indeed come full circle and returned to my family roots.

One difference of opinion with the church emerged after five years. Its locked iron gates were anathema to me. I wanted to make the building more open and welcoming and more widely used, so that local people could feel they 'owned' it. If they came inside the church more often, they might get a more favourable impression and be inclined to join – a significant benefit in face of the rapidly diminishing congregation. However, my suggestion about removing the iron gates met strong resistance because the risk of vandalism and damage was felt to outweigh the advantages.

Despite this, in November 2015 I was finally ordained as an elder in the Non-Subscribing Presbyterian Church. I find this branch of the church to be less judgmental and more open-minded towards other points of view, whilst still being true to Christ's teaching.

The Importance of Music

I loved singing at primary school, but by the time I went to grammar school I found I was too busy with school work, and don't remember any singing apart from at the daily assemblies. But during my nurse training, I found there was a 'Nurses and Doctors Choir', who practised for Christmas concerts and sang carols around the wards on Christmas Eve. Here I started to learn more classical music, such as the Hymn to St Cecilia, and Christmas carols I had never heard before: 'Adam lay y-bounden' and others. I had had a taste of Anglican music while I was assistant matron for a year at Rockport School from September 1963 while waiting to start nurse training, and had accompanied the boys on occasions to the little Church of Ireland at Craigavad. This was a very different form of service to what I had experienced in the Brethren, and I liked it. Especially the music. Though my mother was highly suspicious of the carols to the Virgin Mary!

After I married Chris, we joined a local Presbyterian church, as his family were Presbyterian and I found it an easy way to get away from the Brethren. Most of their hymns were the same, but they had a church choir, and I couldn't wait to join it. Here I learned wonderful descants, and my music-reading skills were put to good use in leading the hymn-singing every Sunday.

After a few years in this church, we moved house to Killinchy, and there I discovered a lovely little choir, The Killinchy Singers. Their leader, Margaret Johnston, was an inspiration to me, and the pieces she chose for us were also ones I loved, mostly classical and liturgical. We performed concerts at Christmas and on other occasions, such as a Candlelit Meditation on the Nativity at Killinchy Non-Subscribing Presbyterian Church (at that time I had no idea what 'non-subscribing' meant). My favourites were 'Break Forth O Beauteous Heavenly Light', 'Panis Angelicus' and 'Quem Pastores'. There were wonderful recitals of sacred music at Down Cathedral and St Mary's Parish Church, Kilmood. The Mozart quartet 'He is Blessed' gave me shivers up and down my spine. And when I sang soprano in the Gibbons quartet 'Almighty and Everlasting God', followed by Purcell's 'Rejoice in the Lord Alway', I felt I had died and gone to heaven!

We lived in Killinchy for about 18 months, from about December 1973 to September 1975, but finding country life with a small baby too restricting, we moved to Holywood and joined a Presbyterian church there. Here we had a succession of very good choirmasters, one standing out above all others: Ronnie Hiscocks. He taught music at the Royal Belfast Academical Institution, and introduced me to more classical and sacred music than I knew existed. The choir grew and grew, and we put on some great concerts and musicals as well as our normal church Sunday music. I learned so much from that man. My pulse would race with sheer enjoyment and praise as we performed in the church, 'The Heavens Declare the Glory of God', and many others. I was also involved in setting up a parent and toddler group in the area.

Sadly, the dynamic of the church changed, and organ music and classic choir material was disdained by a powerful few. There were disagreements and the choirmaster left, to be replaced by other choirmasters who were prepared to go along with the new taste for modern songs but never quite took us to the heights of ecstasy in singing that I had enjoyed so much. I was even accused of being in church only for the music, which did give me some food for thought! Eventually, under pressure, the choir was disbanded, and a 'Praise Group' was formed. I asked to join, but was refused, and after enquiring around, I discovered it was something to do with me as a young widow having an alliance with a man who was attending the church but was separated from his wife. Obviously not a suitable influence for the young people who made up the new praise group!

That and other events led me to leave the church, one being that I had found a new male friend, a widower, who belonged to a nearby Presbyterian church with a great choir and choirmaster. I joined this choir and was back to singing the kind of sacred music I loved – until our musical director was poached by a big city church and moved away to pursue his career there. By then I had joined the Corrymeela Singers, who were connected with the Corrymeela Community and used to put on charity concerts. When this group disbanded, some of us joined the similar choir, Voices Together, which I still enjoy. With age and asthma, my soprano voice has turned alto, but as I read music well I enjoy the mental challenge of learning new songs with new harmonies.

I had put a lot of thought into what the Christian position on sex was, and scoured my Bible and any Christian magazines and books I could find on the subject. Chris and I had been brought up to respect 'The Rule': that sex before marriage was sinful. We managed to keep to it throughout our engagement, though looking back over the years we probably were 'guilty' of the 'Monica Lewinsky' method. But over the years my attitude changed. As a young widow longing for someone to love, the Rule troubled me greatly. It was not a subject I found easy to bring up in conversation with anybody. And then one particular article in a little-known publication, The Irish Christian Digest hit the nail on the head. It was Clifford Longley's paper 'Early Christians had a more robust attitude to sex before marriage', and I found it liberating.

According to Longley, the precept that sex before marriage is wrong 'is commonly singled out as the touchstone of Christian morality'. Yet, he maintains, nothing in the Old or New Testaments says that it is wrong. Moreover, surveys had shown that a large proportion of younger church members were doing it anyway. In fact, 'what is called Christian sexual morality – essentially virginity before marriage in preparation for lifelong monogamy after it – is a social construct which postdates the Bible, and in many respects is relatively modern.' In the Old and New Testaments, female virginity was 'largely a property value: a non-virgin was "damaged goods".' Male virginity had no value at all: polygamy was common and sex was available on demand for slave-owners. Adultery meant sleeping with someone else's wife or fiancée, ie. stealing their goods. St Paul valued virginity 'but as a symbol of dedication to the kingdom of God, not because losing it was especially sinful'.

The sharp line between marriage and non-marriage did not exist in biblical times; it was not introduced in Europe until after the Middle Ages and in England not until 1753. Betrothed couples slept and often lived together. 'Formal blessing by the church was sought only at pregnancy, or even with the birth of a child. Only slowly did church blessing come to be seen as the inauguration of a marriage rather than the confirmation of it... Thus, a medieval Christian marriage began not at a special ceremony, the wedding, but by degrees. There was no sharp line to be crossed, but the existence of the matrimonial bond was deemed to date from the time the couple made a full commitment to each other' – which often happened after they had started sleeping together. 'Folk memory recalls these customs in the expression "common law marriage", and folk are busily reinventing it today. So the idea that sex before marriage is sinful is fairly recent and owes much to the clergy trying to stamp out the pre-1753 notion that marriage is achieved by stages rather than established in public at one moment... But lawyers and churchmen, whose role in the supervision of marriage is thereby weakened, cannot be expected to welcome this. It is not tidy, but neither is human nature.'

I found this article immensely reassuring, as I had been greatly troubled by the conflict between the joy of falling in love and the disapproval of my church. After reading Clifford Longley's article in The Digest, I wrote a letter to another Christian magazine about how enlightening I found it.

I wrote: 'My husband and I followed the Rule with deep angst, but believed it to be right. He died of cancer and years later I fell in love with a widower. Family circumstances made it difficult for us to marry, though we were fully committed to each other. The Dilemma arose again, and after much prayer this article [the Clifford Longley one] appeared in a Christian magazine (no longer being published).

It was like a light from heaven. And while I was looking at it from a widow's perspective, it applies to the broader issue. The next dilemma was the Christian community and how they would accept it. The weaker brother issue bothered me, especially teenagers of which we had five between us! It was a case of honesty when necessary and discretion most of the time. The reason I want this letter printed is that I know so many people from my type of background who have major psychological problems stemming from this rigidity, and I feel it is not necessary! So I would appreciate this side of the argument being presented.

Yours, in search of Christian truth.'

I also spent some time in prayer about the whole issue, and the words of Scripture, 'Trust in the Lord, and he will give thee the desires of thy heart' stood out as I read my Bible. A Christian friend had once asked me what I really wanted in life and what I prayed for for myself. After some thought I said, 'A good job, a suitable husband and a society honouring Christ.'

Fear

Fear ends all reasoning. Throughout my life I have self-checked what drives me or holds me back, and the possibilities that occur to me are love, safety and learning as a way to move forward.

Love is inbred in us all, from the love of our families and later finding someone outside of our family to continue that love. Safety is important, protecting us from harm. Learning means discovering ways to grow and move forward.

However, there is an antithesis to all of these. It is fear. I first met fear when my dad did not arrive as arranged to pick me up from school at the age of six. Back then there was no suggestion of being afraid of 'strangers' and our mobile bread-man took me home. I trusted him, and he delivered me home. The fear of being abandoned was cancelled. I was once more secure in my small family unit.

As I grew older, my Brethren church introduced me to Jesus as a friend who had lived on earth but was now in heaven, waiting for the time he would return to take those he loved there with him. Some children became fearful that, if they didn't love him enough, their parents could be taken to heaven and leave them behind. So I bit the bullet and committed my young self to him – and that fear was dealt with. I innocently believed the interpretation I had been given, and for the time being it solved the problem.

The next time I considered the subject of fear was after reading about the martyrs who were burned to death for their faith. It seemed unlikely this would happen in our little Christian country, so I decided I could dismiss that fear. Then, after having children, I heard talk in the news of nuclear war, and as a parent I was now in protective mode. So I did a bit of reading and concluded that the possibility was on a low scale. At this point I decided to ask myself what else I might be afraid of, and after some consideration I decided I was secure in a loving family and a country that provided me with education and enough money to live fairly comfortably.

Years passed and, even when I was hit hard by bereavement, the God I trusted provided for all my earthly needs through the life insurance my husband had sensibly provided. I coped as a widow, and my children grew up healthy and fearless, and left home each in their own sphere of development, which in all three cases involved the internet. And this is the point where I, as a pretty fearless female, looked into the risks involved from hacker attacks and privacy issues, followed the prescribed paths and moved on. By 2010 I had remarried, was coping with my new husband's dementia, and was now a Facebook user. Again, aware of the risks of scamming and trolls, I faced these fears, befriending a Facebook user who wrote horrible things about Christian churches. Treating him on a friendly basis, I discovered an interesting man with a lot of anger, and later he apologised for the things he had said about my church.

And now that Paul has passed on, and I am a widow again, I have sometimes felt lonely, but Holywood friendships, our Oxfam shop, church and U3A have been good outlets for activities for me. The year Paul died, I made a new friendship with a man who had a slightly similar history to me. Born in Holywood and educated by the Christina Brothers in Dublin, Gerry was raised as a Roman Catholic but converted to the Protestant faith when he was 19 through a preacher called Hedley Murphy. Gerry joined the Brethren the following year. An ex-policeman, now retired and no longer with the Brethren, he had come out as gay after his marriage failed. He joined the Holywood Mens Shed to pursue his love of woodturning, later becoming a member of the Irish woodturners guild. But following a disagreement with some people in the Men's Shed, he had to leave. He was devastated as he then had nowhere to pursue his hobby. So I suggested he use my garage, which Paul had set up as a workshop. Gerry was delighted to accept, and for me it was good to have a male friend around to share a coffee and help with odd jobs.

I found that Gerry knew his Bible well, and we became good friends, nothing more. He attends my church, the non-subscribing branch of the Presbyterian church, and the whole subject of homosexuality was discussed. I had previously become convinced through Ikon, Corrymeela and various friends that homosexuality was not a sin, as my church also believed. Recently, the Presbyterian Church in Ireland had reached a decision to deny communion or baptism of infants to gay church members. We explored whether Biblical texts actually supported this view, and were happy to take a stance with the Non-Subscribers that this was not the will of a loving God.

It has been good for both of us to develop this friendship, and I thank God for his provision as I get older and less able, with arthritis problems increasing.

And that's where I'm at now! Past the three score and ten, with some health struggles – notably the return of arthritis, which my GP hoped had 'burnt itself out'. I am now with another doctor and back on my tablets. But all things considered, I am happy and confident as I enter the last stage of the journey.

Theme Park for Northern Ireland

It was on a visit to Paris some years ago that the inspiration struck me. Parc Asterix was based around the story of Asterix the Gaul, which I had avidly consumed from the comic books as a child. At the theme park, local cultural influences were used to inform the youngsters visiting the park about their own local heritage. And I started thinking, what if we had a park like this in Northern Ireland?

I started there and then to write down the ways this idea could be developed. I thought about the stories and the people I'd read about in Irish culture. St Patrick, Mary Ann McCracken, the giants of the Giants Causeway, the Pirate Queen, Niall of the Nine Hostages... Some people's stories were based in Northern Ireland, others further south or across the border in County Donegal. I wrote it all down and wondered how it could be developed. The first place I approached was Bryson House in Belfast, where my proposal was read and praised as a brilliant idea, but they suggested I should work on a business plan. And there was astonishment that a nurse (as I was then) could create an imaginative plan such as this. I felt honoured, and started finding out about business plans. Sadly, I was to discover this was not my forte!

The idea lay in a cupboard for years. Then in 2017, I noticed a request from Belfast City Council for ideas on uses for the area called The Giants Park, an area of reclaimed land on the western shore of Belfast Lough. I contacted the council, and their Property and Projects officer Sabine Kalke invited me to take a tour of the site and discuss my ideas. Sabine felt EU or council funding might be available, and referred me via the Go-For-It programme to business advisers who might help do the business plan. Sabine and the business advisers were all enthusiastic.

This, in outline, was my idea:

A THEME PARK FOR BELFAST 2017 … IMAGINE…!

The vision:

- To enable all residents of Ireland, especially those in the north, to find a way to really enjoy all the cultural benefits of our shared heritage, in a relaxed and pleasurable setting.

- To attract the European and international communities to a place where they can see and enjoy the many benefits of our beautiful island.

- To channel our varying cultural aspirations in a harmless and positive way.

- To encourage a pride in our common cultural heritage.

- To stimulate a more light-hearted approach to our national life.

The plan:

- A Theme Park similar to Parc Asterix in France.

- Full of visual, aural, tasteful and sensitive images attracting all ages.

- Making expansive use of the many stories from both Catholic and Protestant as well as pre-reformation culture.

- Put together using modern technology and natural materials.

•Integrating the warm-hearted and generous nature of the (northern) Irish people.

The benefits

•Enabling local (northern) Irish people to mix freely in a relaxed and non-threatening, non-defensive setting. Then perhaps even without realising, they may find out about other cultures in their own society. In so doing they may then discover how much they actually have in common, and how little they need to be threatened by others. And perhaps they can then learn to laugh a little at themselves, and eventually reach out to those they have previously felt suspicious of or hurt by.

•Offering massive employment opportunities.

•Promoting a national feeling of self-worth and pride in our combined heritage.

•Promoting more international understanding and interest in this beautiful country.

•Enabling us to be more positive and creative in how we as a country spend international and European money.

I went on to develop ideas under copyright about what attractions and educational themes to include. As an update on the Giants Park theme park from September 2018, it has just been announced on radio that a theme park is to be built on the site I had been shown. Sponsorship now seems available from Belfast City Council and Peace Money, and they are just waiting for a company to apply to build it, at which point my idea can be offered to them. It will be years before it actually opens but, if and when it does, it will be my legacy to my home city.

Victoria Memorial Hall, May St, Belfast

With Mary McAleese at her home, Aras an Uachtarain, near Dublin

The real purpose of religion is permanent astonishment

One God. combining our faiths in a simple message

CONCLUSION

The River of My Life

Looking back, I sometimes think my life is like a river. And it occurs to me, when God created rivers, he did not make them go straight from the mountain to the sea like the canals that man makes. He created them to meander and sometimes double back in great horse-shoe curves. My small trickle that started in the mountains was fed along the way by the influence of the many people who impacted on my life – my friends, relatives, Sunday school and day school teachers, etc. And so I began to grow into an adult river, usually flowing stronger as it went, but sometimes held back by obstacles or changing to a trickle as events around affected its course.

Rivers and streams can run through marshy places, swamps or mud fields. These represented to me times of illness or sadness. Their course can be altered by obstacles, or they can become polluted and muddied. When healthy they can support life, both plant and animal. My river flowed through all of these.

There had been obstacles in my early life – my mother's nervous illness created a marshy area, but later I found direction in my nursing career, which introduced me to new channels of thought and gave me confidence to explore the world around.

Meeting my husband Chris was the point where my river began to flow alongside another stream, and together we became strong. He was the biggest single human influence in my life. With children we became part of the wider world of families and friends, forming delightful pools of relationship, places to swim and share our lives. Life was a joy until tragedy hit in the form of serious illness: a huge boulder, thrown into the middle of the strong stream, causing turbulence and fear. We floundered around, grabbing for any rocks that would support us: healing services, prayer, doctors, friends. But sadly, this strong river was split in two. The part that was Chris trickled away to nothing, as he was absorbed into God and eternity. When he died, the river narrowed to a smaller stream, but was soon joined by other stronger streams – friends and family. Other relationships somewhat muddied the waters, until I found one that gave support to the frequent trickles that previously had seemed to just turn to mud. And my relationship with God became again like the river bank, providing strength, security, integrity and meaning, especially in times of trouble. The stream that was me had difficulty finding this river bank, but when it did, it stayed close to it, and because it was a strong bank, the river grew strong again. The stream that was Chris returned to me in dreams and seemed to be always there in a part of my consciousness.

River of my Life

StoryTerrace

PEACEANGEL'S WHITE FEATHERS

Story Terrace helps people capture personal stories in beautiful books alongside a professional writer.
www.storyterrace.com

StoryTerrace

StoryTerrace

48110335R00157

Printed in Poland
by Amazon Fulfillment
Poland Sp. z o.o., Wrocław